Dark Visions
SELECTED PAINTINGS
BY TIFFANY TOLAND-SCOTT

Dark Visions
by Tiffany Toland-Scott
First Published April 2018
Published by TitoLand
ISBN: 978-0692099247

Special Thanks

This book is dedicated to Angie Felter.
Her support of my art and this project made this book a reality.
From the bottom of my heart, thank you, Angie.

A Note from the Artist

Selecting the work for this book was quite an undertaking. Those
of you familiar with my work may find that your favorite
pieces are missing. After producing close to 1,000 pieces of art
over the years, whittling it down to just a few favorites
was a difficult task, and unfortunately I've had to
leave out some of my popular gothic paintings.

This book represents a collection of my most popular pieces, my
own personal favorites, and pieces that I felt were landmarks
in my progression as an artist.

HAUNTING MELODY

2009

I grew up deep in the woods of the Cascade Mountains. Surrounded by lakes, swamps, and marshes, my childhood was full of ghost stories and strange sounds in the woods. One of the strangest things I encountered were orbs of floating light, and the sound of voices murmuring in the woods.

Eventually I learned that the lights were swamp lights, and the murmuring voices were tiny brooks that emerged each spring and dried up in the summer heat. But I can't help but be reminded of them whenever I read a folktale about faeries leading travelers astray in the woods.

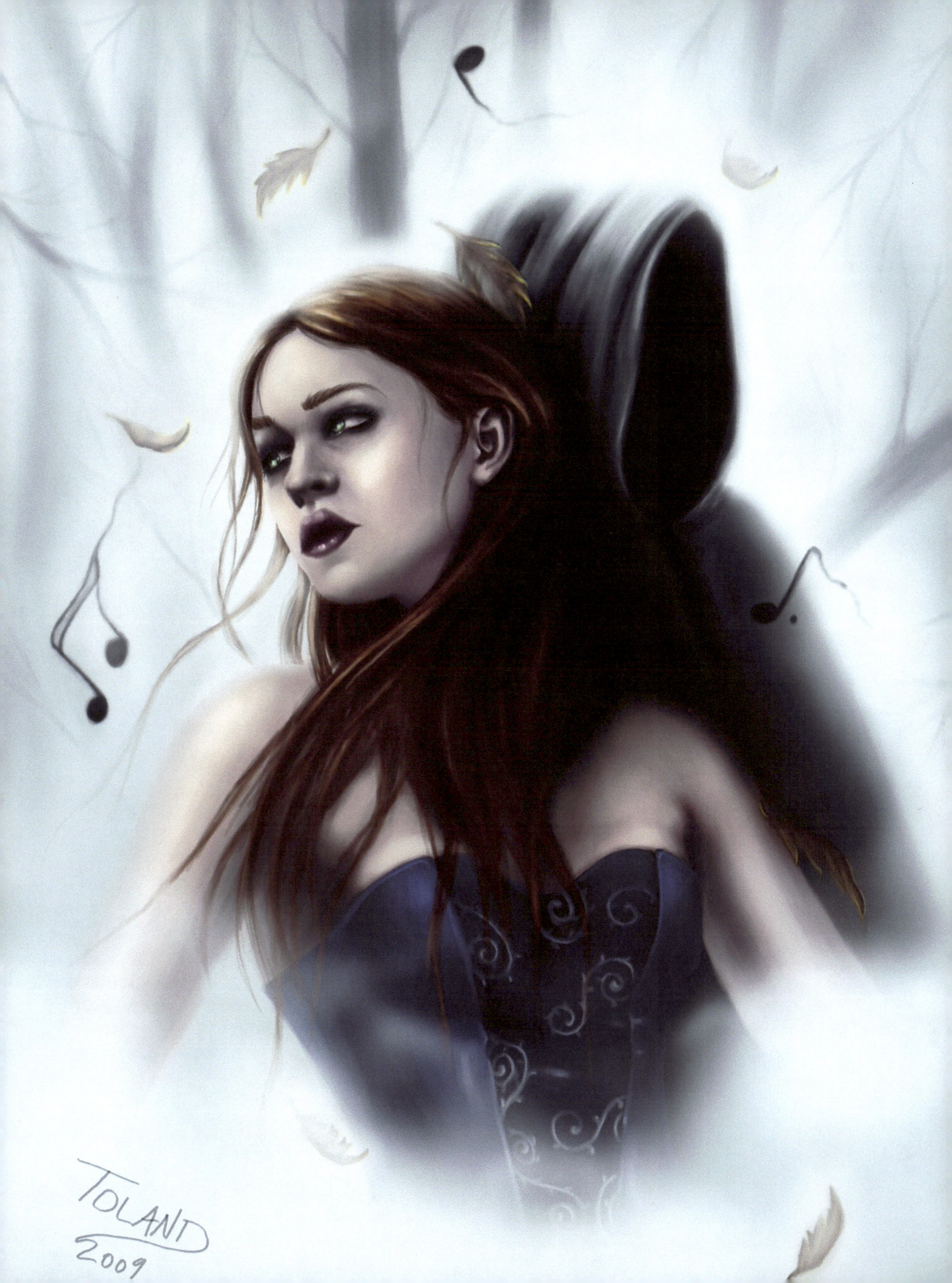

ROWENA'S ALTAR
2013

A few years ago I came up with an idea for a graphic or illustrated novel that I wanted to write and illustrate. My love of classic fairy tales and my desire to give them a darker and more modern twist led me to the concept, and I was all fired up to finish it as quickly as possible.

It was at that time that I had started to shift towards working in oils, though, and soon I couldn't stand to paint on the computer anymore. I didn't want the art to be disjointed, so I decided I would start over in oils, or force myself to finish it digitally. Then life and other projects got in the way, and I didn't have a chance to try either option.

Maybe someday soon I'll make a choice and finish the work.

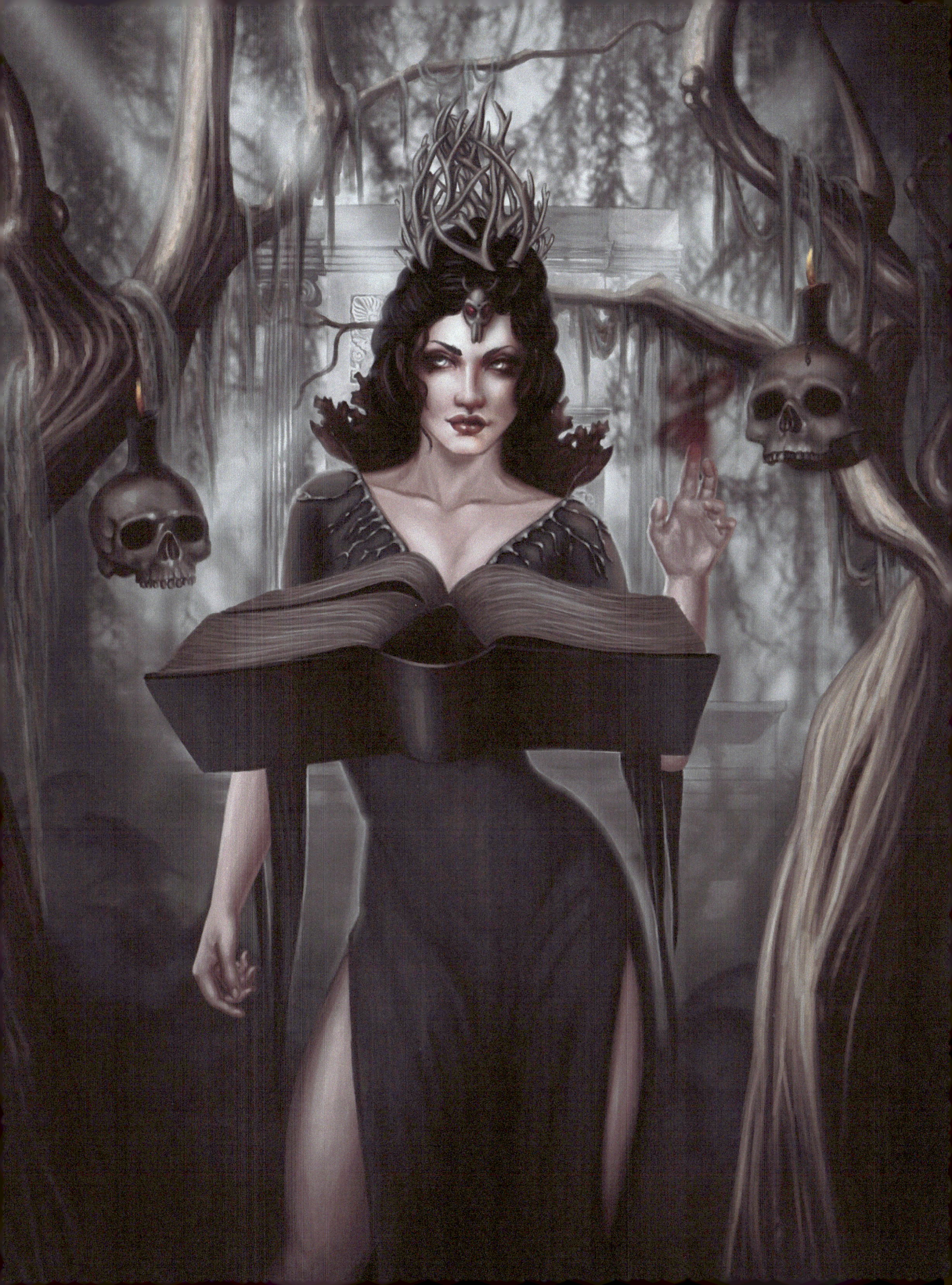

LUPA

2010

I love dogs. I also love cats, but I can't imagine life without dogs. My dog Mythri has been with me since the beginning of 2010 and has been my constant companion ever since.

I wanted to paint a Wolf Goddess, although I am not sure if one really exists. It seems a bit sad that man's best friend doesn't have a major player in humanity's vast pantheon.

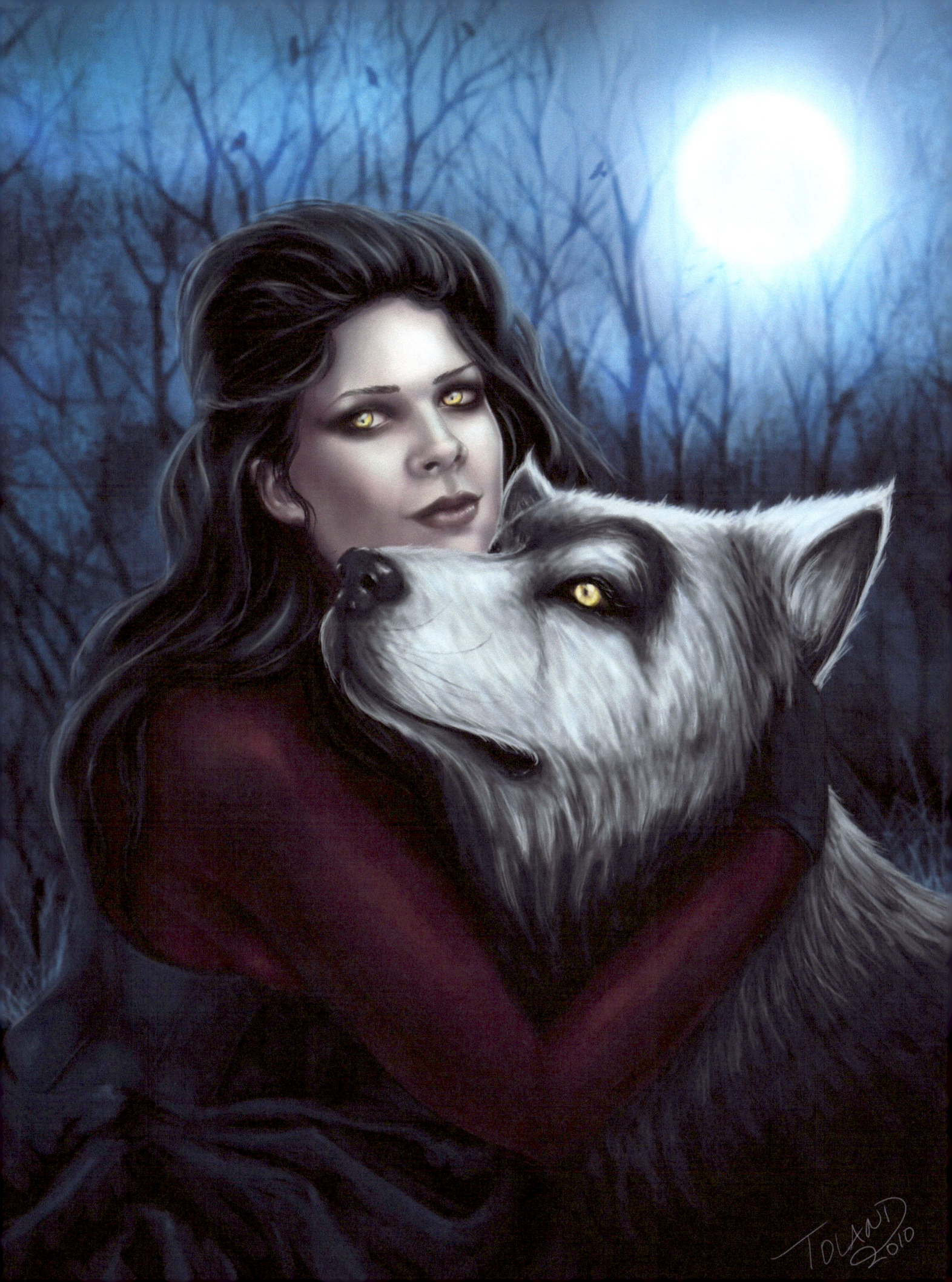

MIRROR, MIRROR

2005

I love evil stepmothers, sorceresses, wicked witches, the whole nasty-magic-lady trope, all of it! It doesn't matter to me if it's the witch from Sleeping Beauty, the stepmother from Snow White, or the Wicked Witch of the West, I'd be all of those before I'd be some fainting princess.

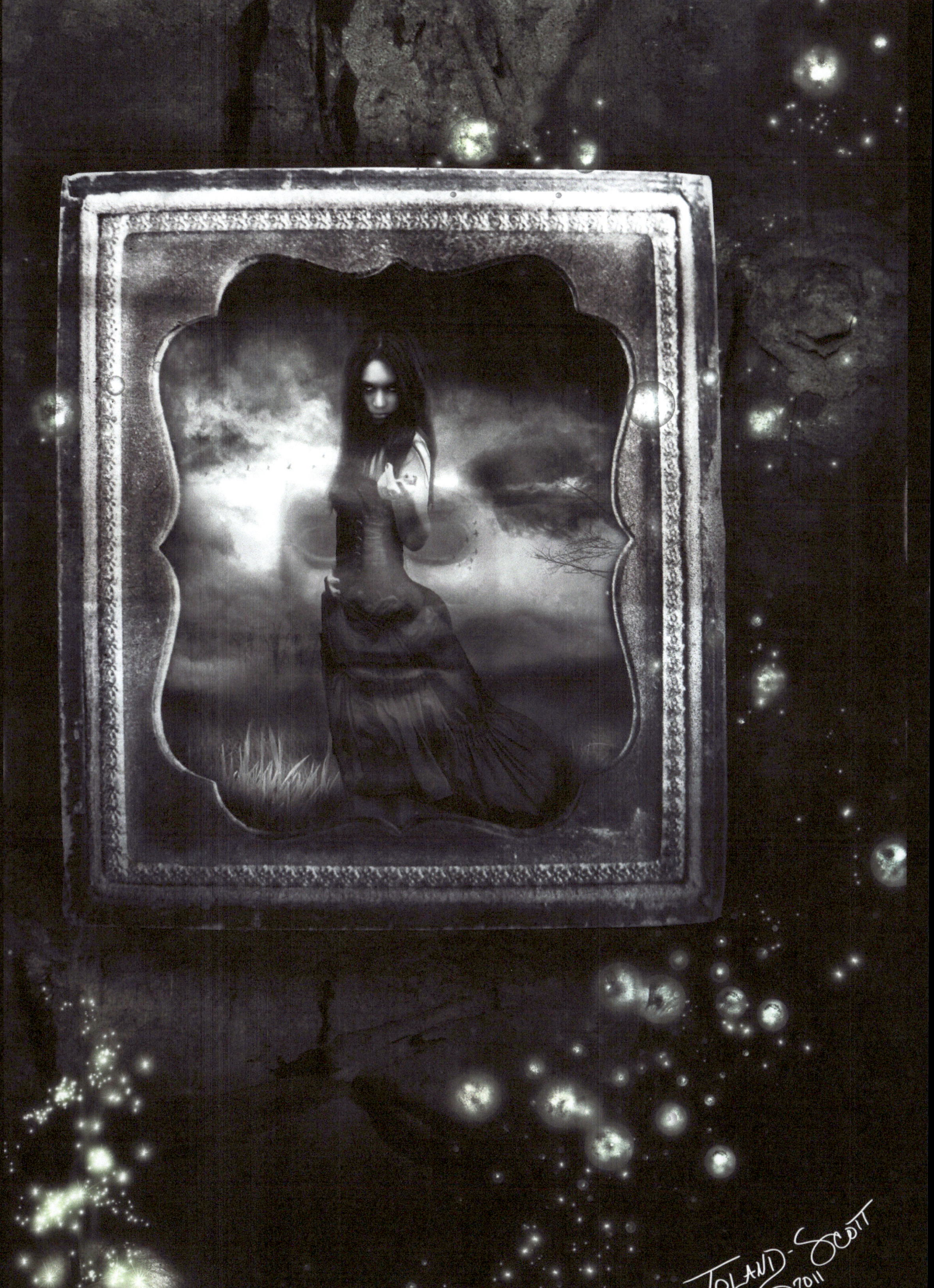

SPIDERBAIT

2014

It feels like spiders are attracted to me for some mysterious spider-y reason. I am always finding them around my workspace no matter where I live. They even seem to be attracted to my temporary workspaces when I am traveling and working on the road.

I used to be extremely arachnophobic but over the years I've learned to live with them. I would even say that some spiders are nice to have around. I may not have come around until I saw a spider eating a mosquito in my studio, but eventually I came around.

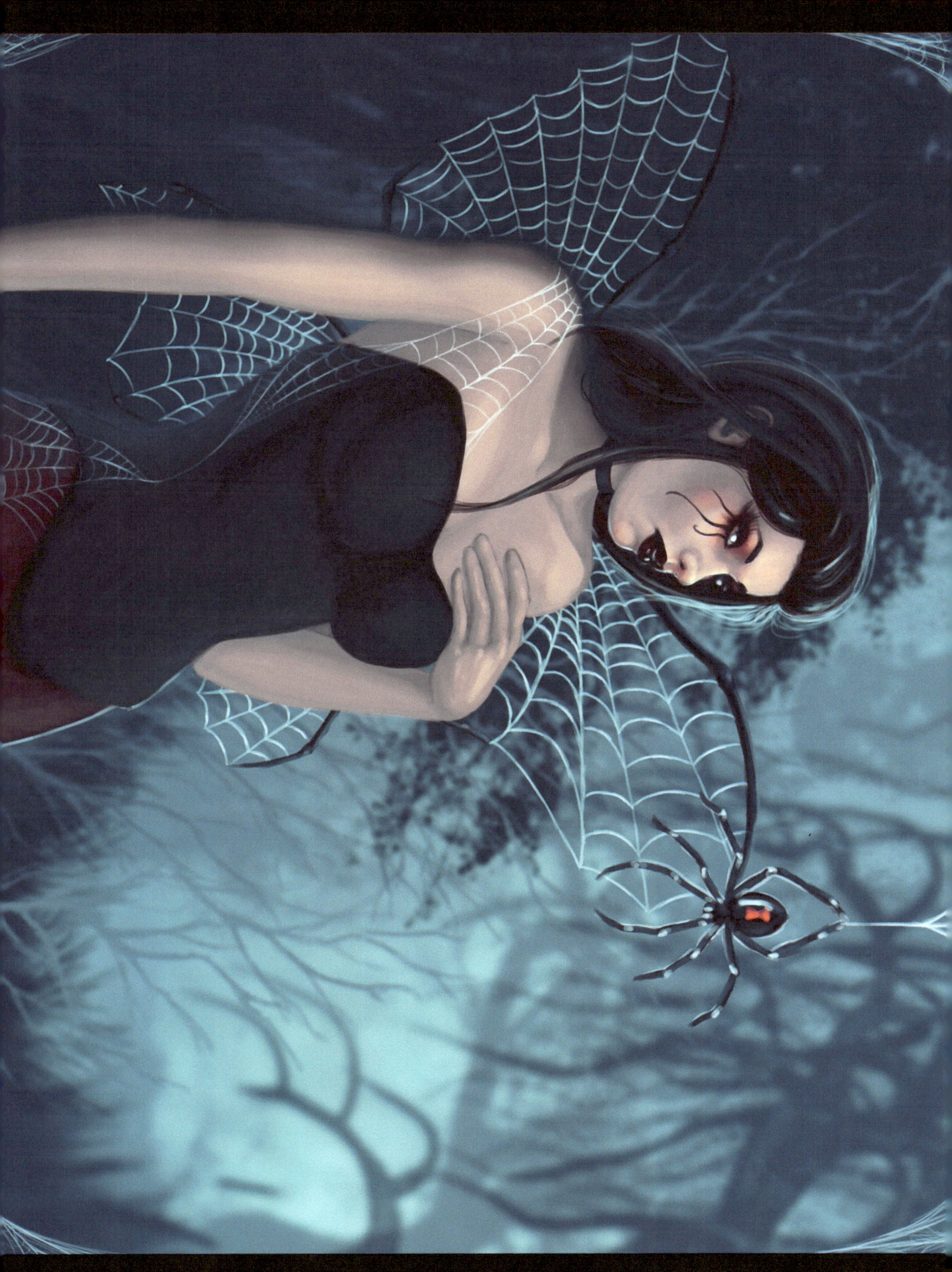

THE WILL-O-THE-WISP

2012

When I was a little girl I lived in the Wenatchee National Forest near a lake called Lake Cle Elum (it means "swift water"). Some of the areas around the lake were marshy and marked with trails and driftwood. These were my favorite places to play, in the tall grasses and tangles of dead branches. Sometimes I would spot an orb of light, usually green, on the other side of the lake. Not having a boat or a great swimming ability, I was never able to investigate the source of the lights and my imagination ran wild.

Later on, as a young adult, I learned of the phenomenon of "willow wisps", which ancient peoples believed were fairies. People who saw them often wandered off after them and fell into bogs or otherwise met an untimely demise.

Now we know it's swamp gas… or is it?

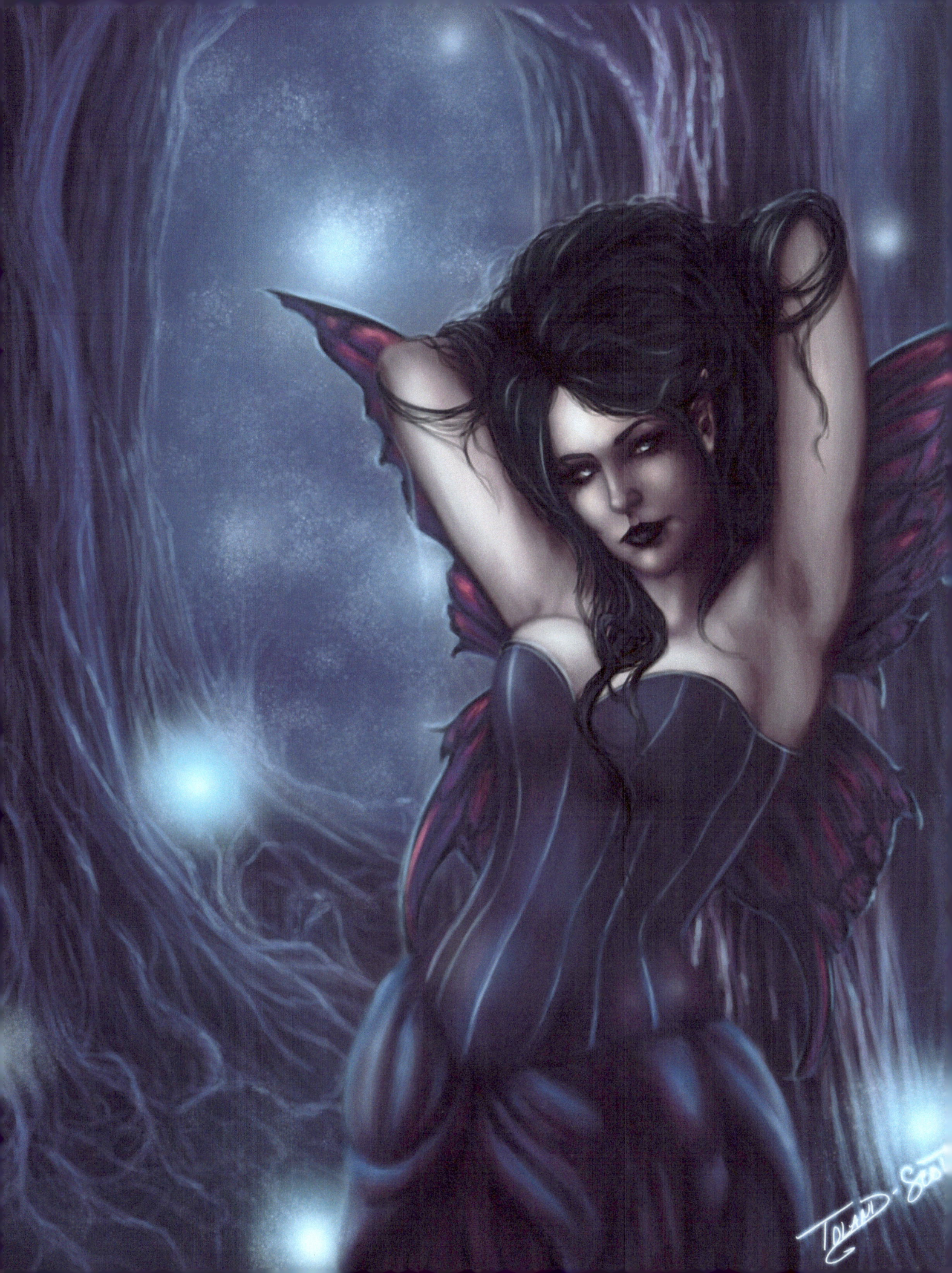

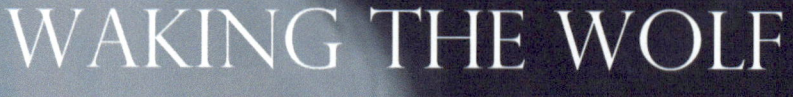

WAKING THE WOLF
2009

For a long while I thought I would get into game art
and be a game artist. It never really happened but that didn't
stop me from producing a small portfolio of art that
I planned to use to approach game companies.
I ended up selling prints of the pieces instead, so it wasn't
a waste of time, and painting this werewolf was truly
a lot of fun.

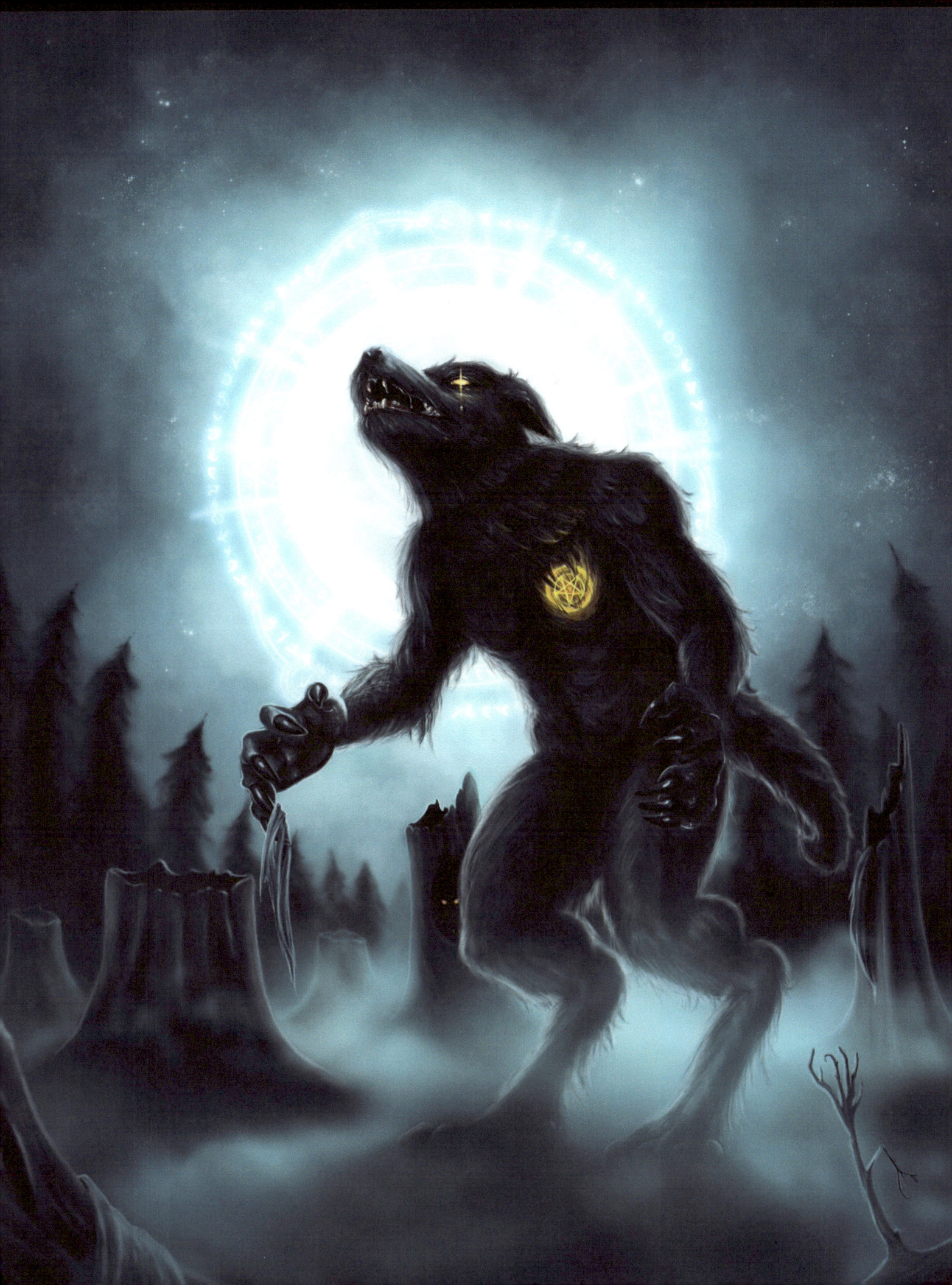

A ROSE IN THE RAIN

2007

In 2007, I enrolled in art school for the first time. I was initially pursuing a degree in multimedia, or game design, and I figured that's what I would do with the rest of my life. My art frequently mirrors my life, and as my art took a dark turn, so did my life. Not long after I completed this piece, disillusioned and disenchanted with the for-profit art school industry, I would leave my degree program, enroll in another, and then leave school behind entirely.

These days I warn young artists to avoid for-profit art schools like art institutes and other private colleges. Nobody should have to pay $80,000 or more for a decent art education.

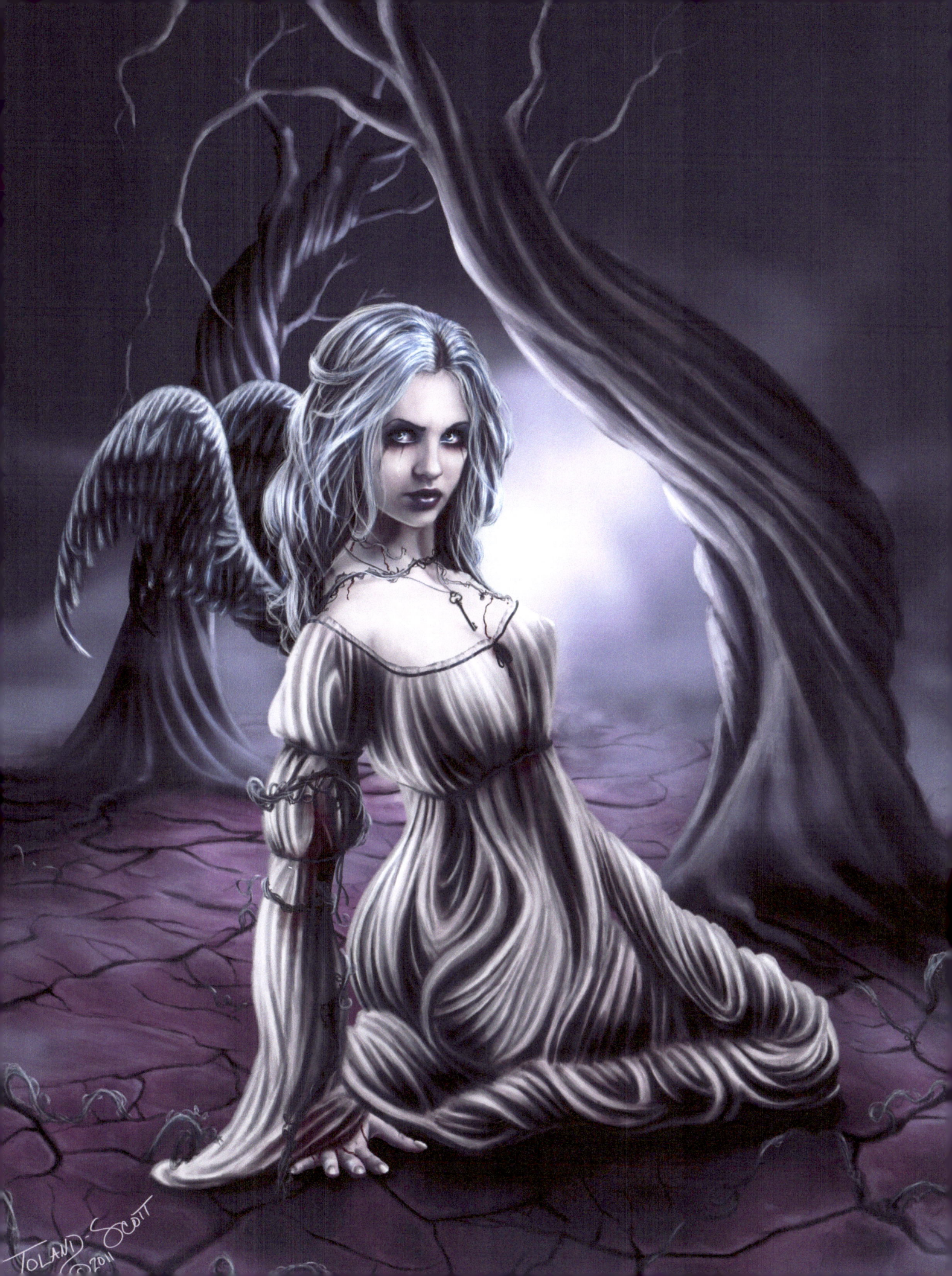

DEATH
2012

I painted Death and Rebirth to go together as a set, but as
ever, it seems many people are attracted to one or the other
and rarely both. It's funny how it often works out that way.

I often paint in the theme of opposites or light and dark.
These two pieces were both inspired by the beautiful scenery
of Highgate Cemetery in London, England.

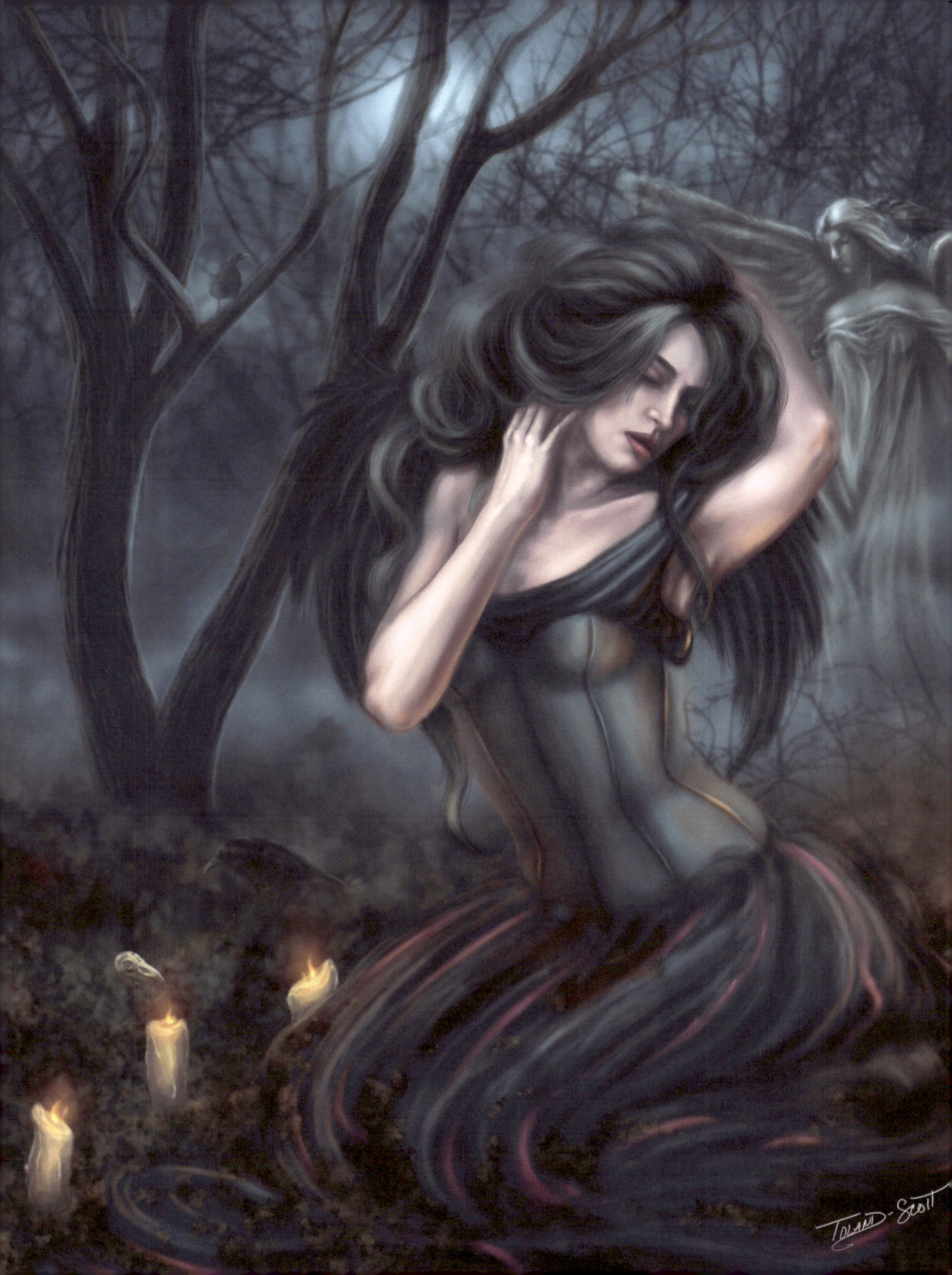

REBIRTH

2012

I painted "Rebirth" in the springtime and "Death" naturally
followed in the autumn. My work often features
symbols of rebirth and renewal. I always look forward
to spring and the promise of mornings in the garden.
"Rebirth" is ultimately a painting about my love of
gardening and collecting plants.
I am always looking for new additions and seeking out
mysterious green spaces, like old cemeteries and
abandoned gardens.

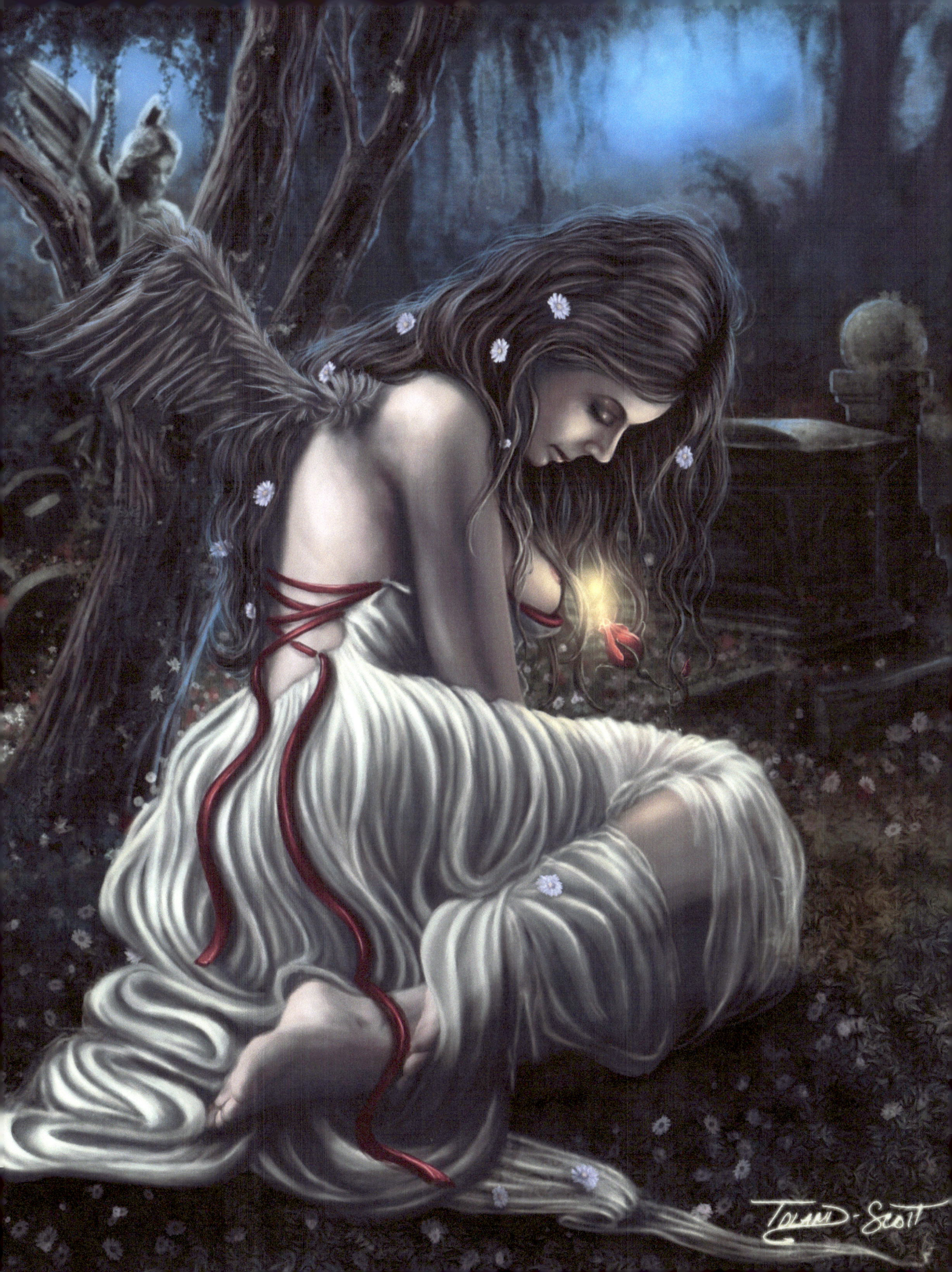

STAGE FRIGHT

2008

Puppets and antique dolls are a bit of a recurring theme for me. I don't always show the works that I create surrounding them. Sometimes they're too personal and I just think no one would understand them.

Stage fright is one of those things that I think most people "get", however. It doesn't really matter who you are, or if getting on stage is part of your job.
Stage fright eventually hits just about everyone.

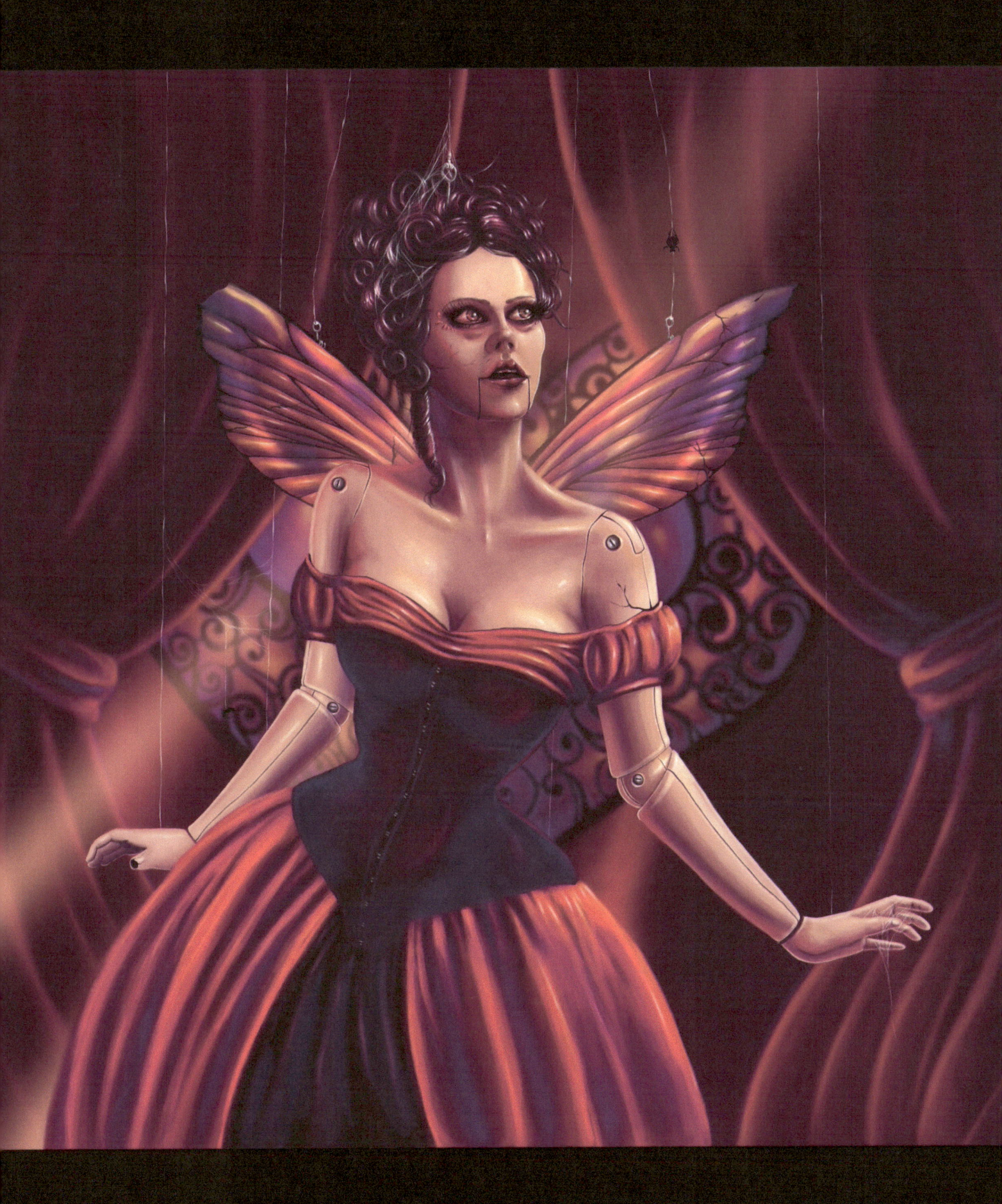

WINTER SOUL

2010

I must have a winter spirit. It seems like I really "come alive"
when the weather starts to cool off.
Paintings fly out of my fingertips like snow in a blizzard
and yet somehow I don't have enough time to paint all
the things that pop into my head every time I look
out the window.

When I was younger I used to really love the snow.
Now, as an adult, I'm not such a fan of that cold "stuff",
but I can't deny the spell of inspiration it seems
to cast over me.

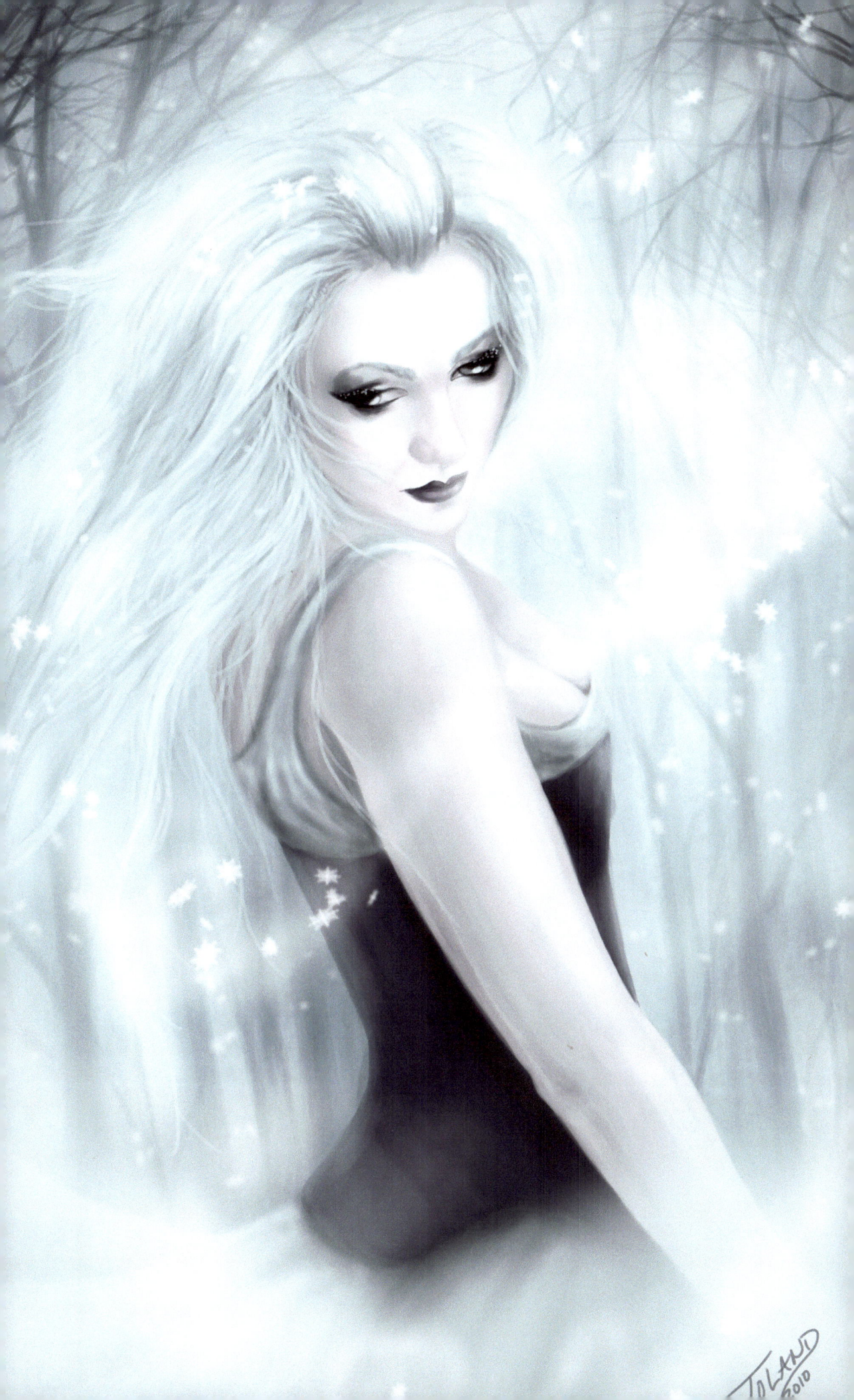

A WARNING

2010

It's no secret to fans of my art that I have a penchant for classic vampires. I love vampires in general, but classic vamps are just more fun to paint. From their period clothing to the beautiful Victorian cemeteries they're often associated with, classic vampires remain one of my favorite subjects to paint.

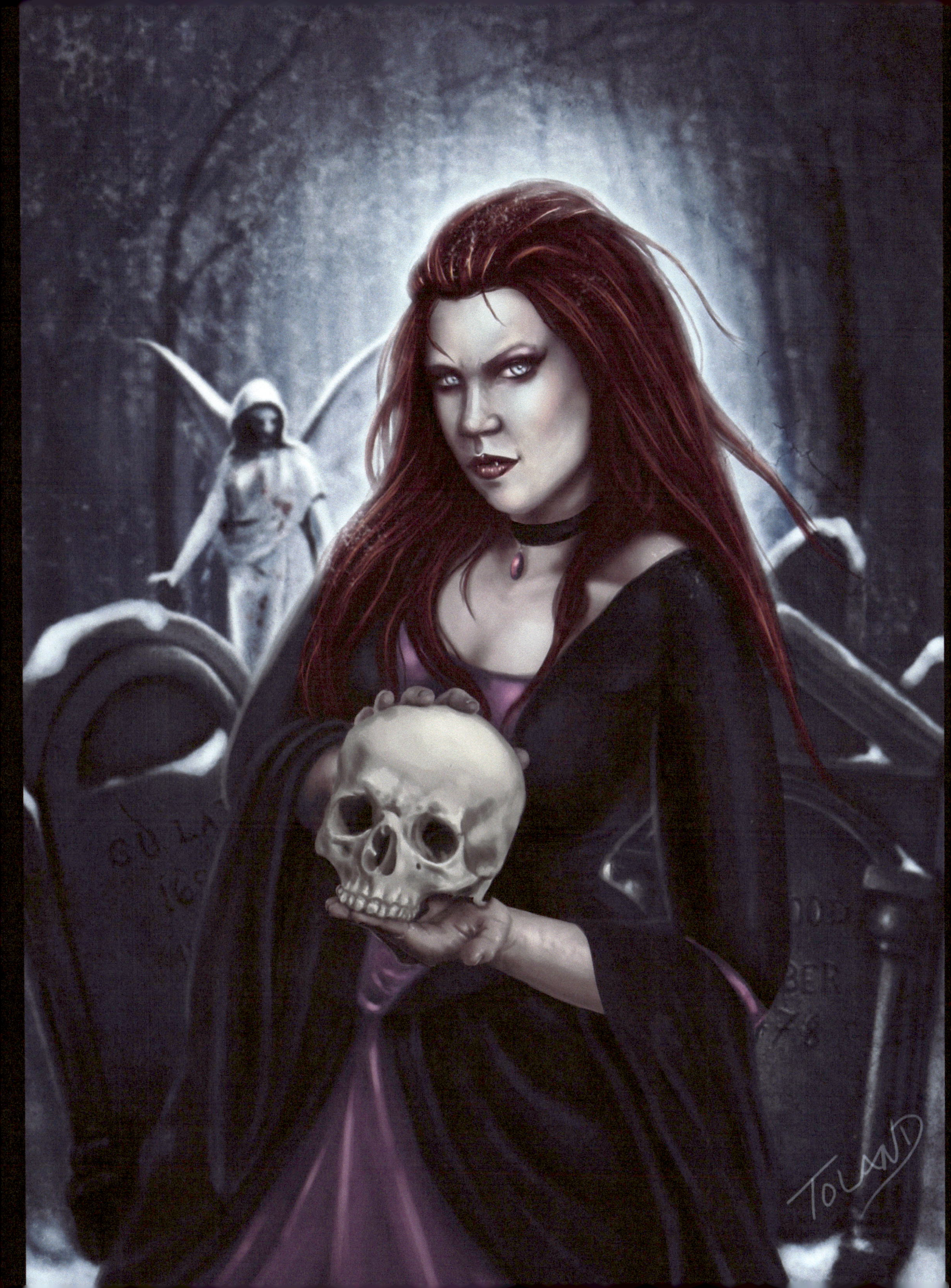

BLUEBOTTLE

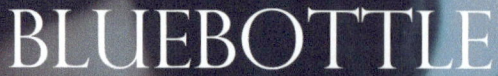

2014

I did not intend for this fairy to be as darkly surreal as she
ended up. The other two butterfly fairies I painted
to go with ended up being quite cute and even girly.
This one on the other hand… I don't think she can
be trusted…

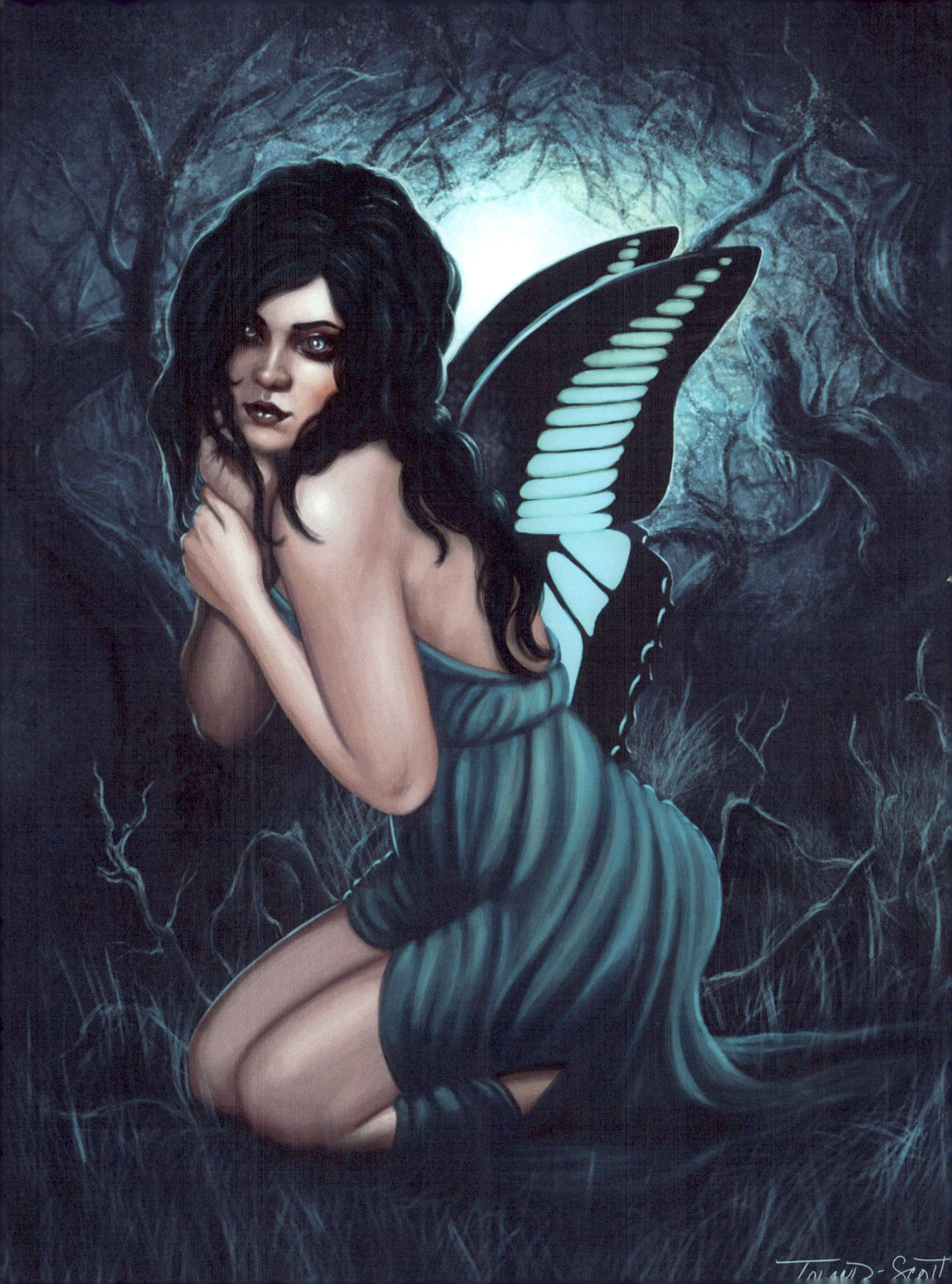

CALL OF THE MORRIGHAN

2012

In Irish mythology, The Morrighan is a war goddess associated with death in battle. Her functions as a goddess are tied up in fate and foretelling doom, as she was sometimes a symbol of a soldier's imminent, violent death. However, she was also believed to influence the outcome of wars, as she would appear in the form of a crow flying over the battlefield, either to strike fear or courage into the hearts of the soldiers below.

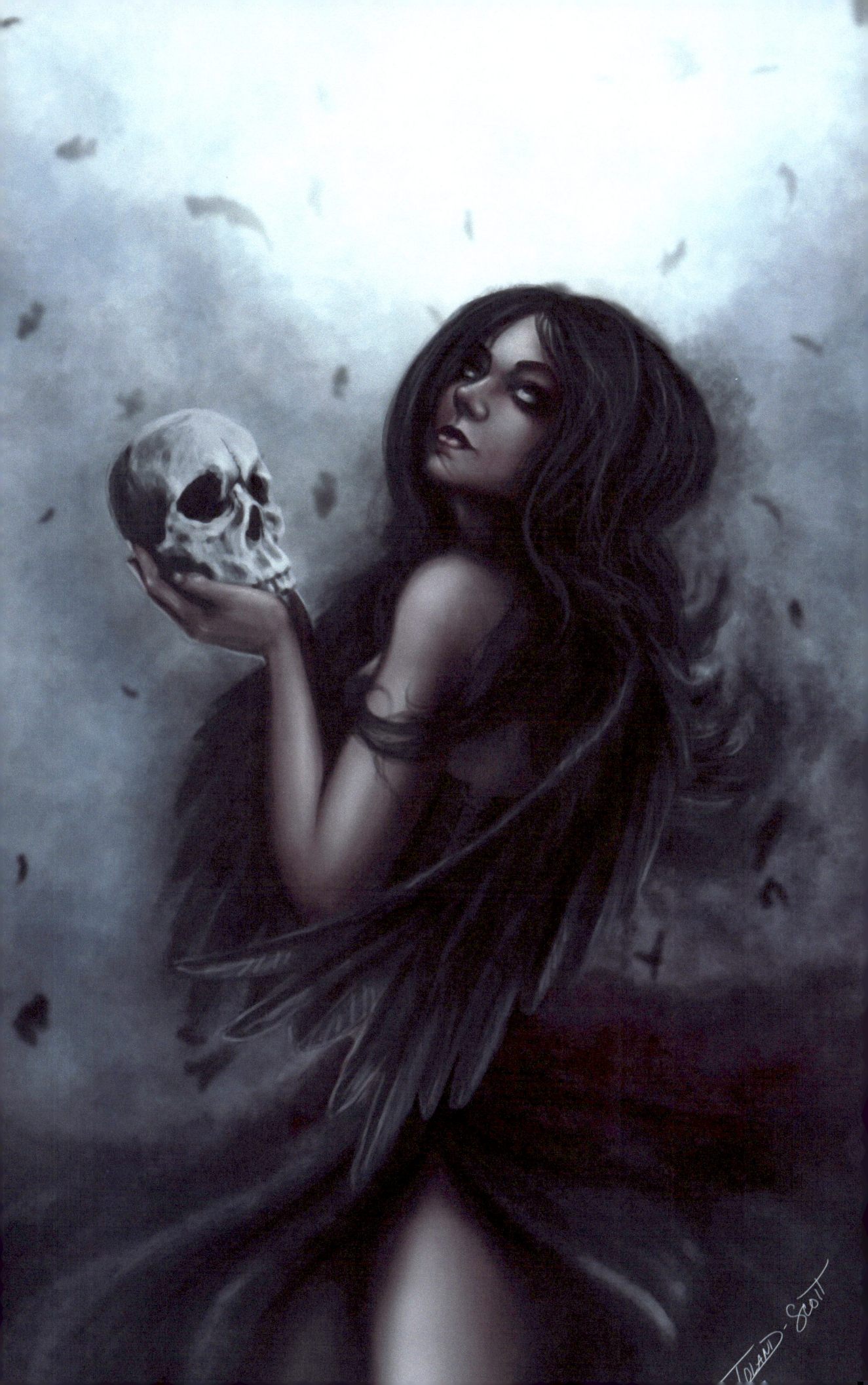

EVANESCENCE

2005

This piece was a combination of many techniques -
photo manipulation, photography, and digital painting. I was
nearing the end of my experiments in photo manipulation
when I created this piece, and had begun painting more and
more and relying on photographs less and less.

Rather obviously this piece was inspired by the band
Evanescence, but also the definition of the word evanescence.
I love ghost stories and anything darkly romantic, and I feel
like this piece really captured everything I've ever hoped to
capture in my art.

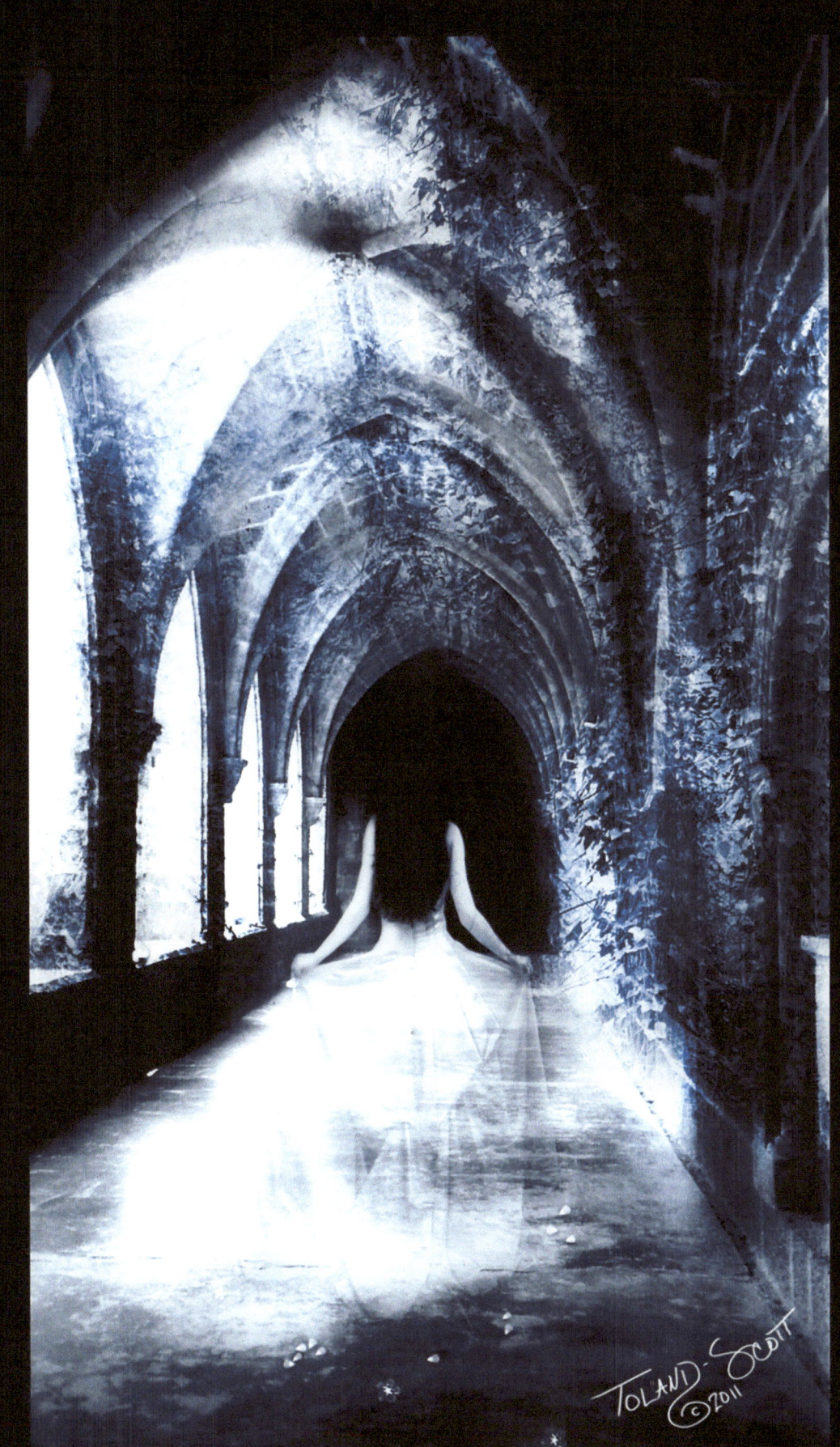

Toland-Scott ©2011

HARMONY OF NIGHT

2012

Back in 2005, I first created this piece as a combination of
photo manipulation and digital painting. It was very small and
had a low-resolution, but it was one of my favorite pieces at
the time.

In 2012 I decided to recreate her, but I still prefer the version
from 2005, which you can see in the background of this text.
There was something about the original that I just couldn't
capture in digital paint back then.

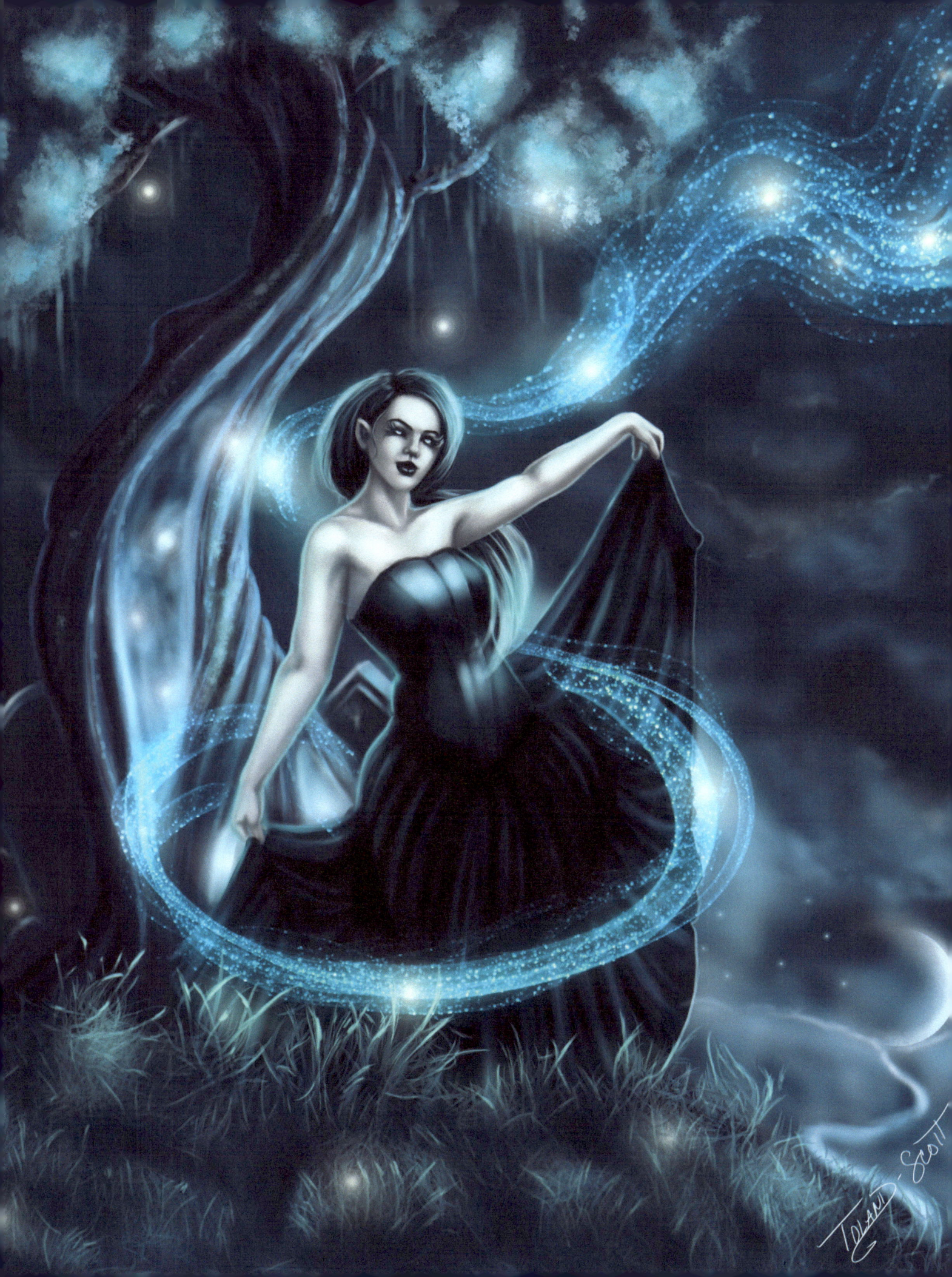

EVIL QUEEN COMPLEX
2012

I think we all know, or have known, an "Evil Queen". Or perhaps we've all been an "Evil Queen" at least once in our lives. I've always identified more with the evil queens in fairy tales - after all, they have magic and what does Snow White have? Singing dwarves and woodland critters?

Gag me with a spoon.

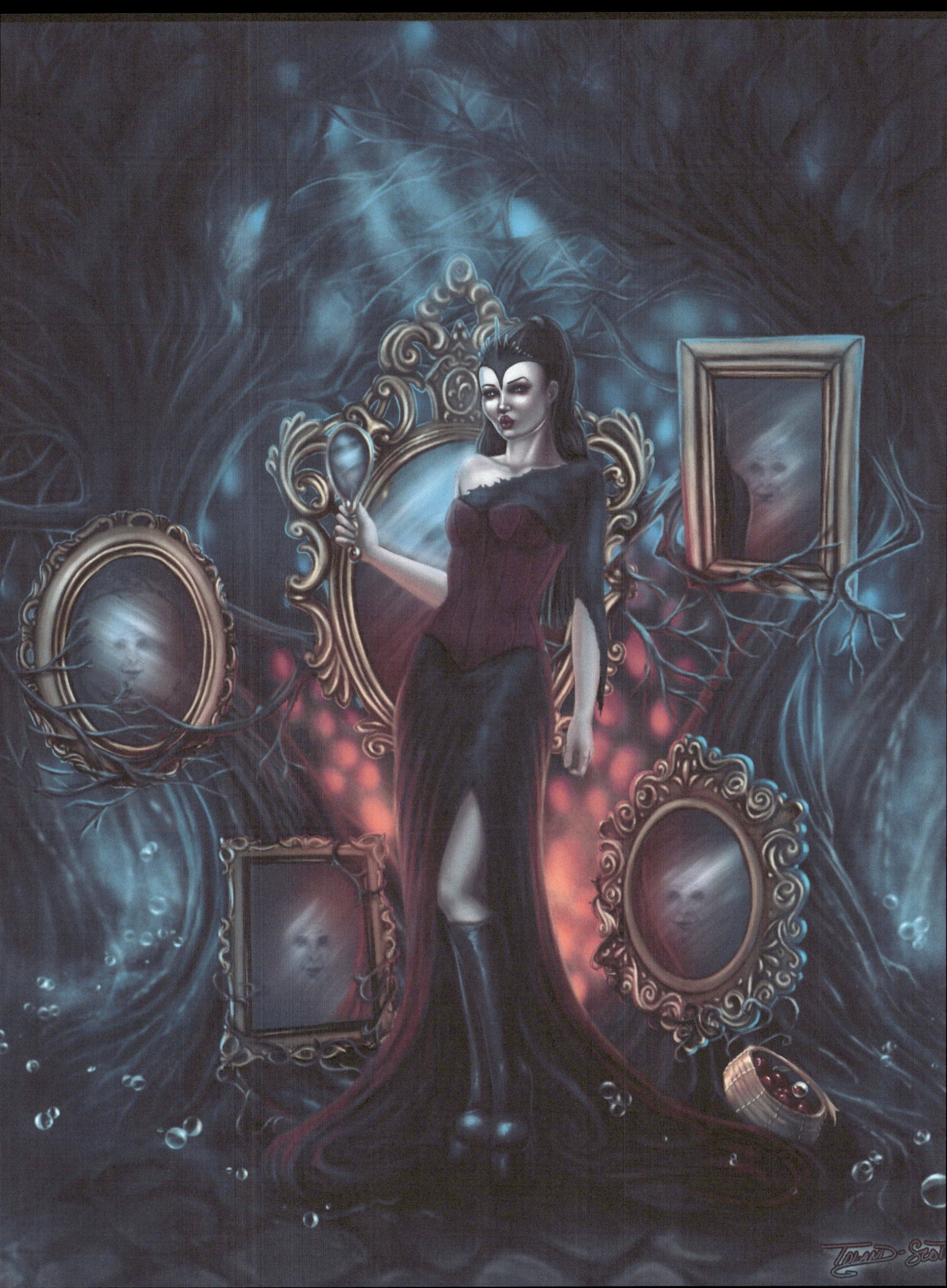

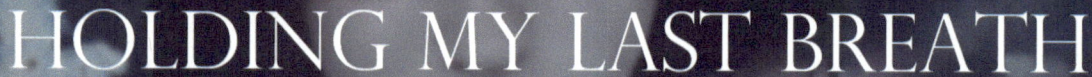

HOLDING MY LAST BREATH
2005

I've always been fascinated with dark Ophelia-like characters. She makes a great art subject, an opinion which many other artists must share, given the staggering number of Ophelia paintings that exist in the world today.

This particular piece was a combination of photographs, digital painting, and photographic manipulation or photo editing. I was very successful with this technique, but it was very restrictive in many ways, and I felt I could never fully express myself in this medium.

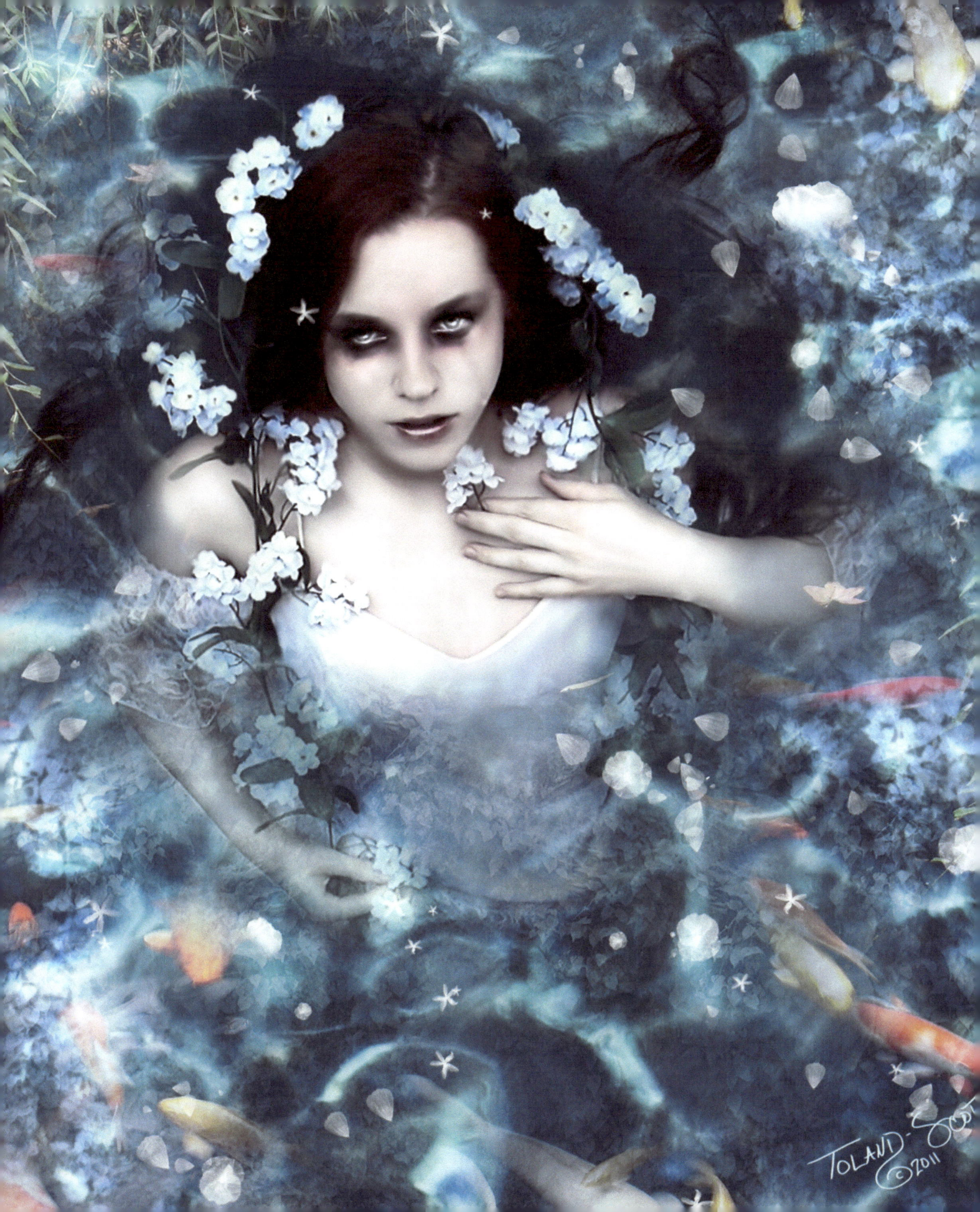

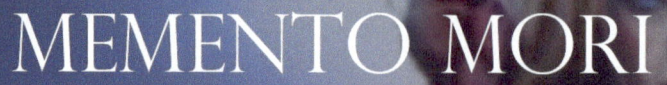

MEMENTO MORI
2010

A sweet little gothic fairy to remind you that you're mortal.
That is all "memento mori" means - remember you
have to die.

We don't get a choice, and we usually don't know when
it will happen. Don't waste your time on things
that don't matter. You can't take material things
with you when you go. So do whatever fills your spirit
up with joy. Don't bother pursuing the things
that don't make your heart sing.

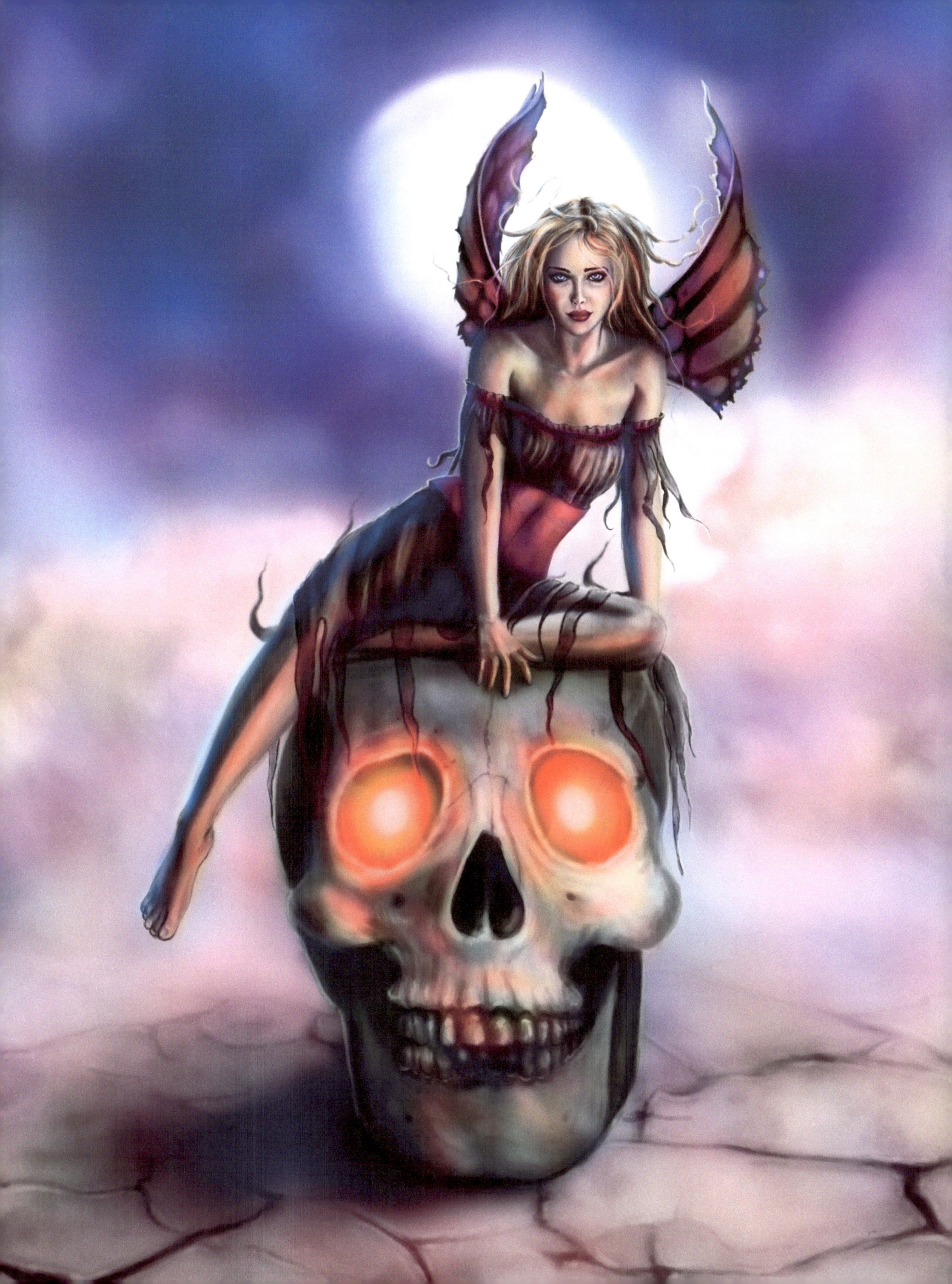

THE WITCHING H OUR

2012

I used to have a cat named Kerwin, but I called him Kirby.
Life had not been kind to him before I found him
at a shelter, a matted mass of orange fur curled up in the
back of a cage. I knew I had to take him home the instant I
saw him.

He hated everyone and everything, except for me. He
followed me all around the house and rarely ever
left my side. He never learned to like other people and
as old age and senility set in he no longer even tolerated the
presence of anyone else.

Eventually the senility took him over
the Rainbow Bridge and that was the end
of my constant companion.

I painted this spectral cat one year after he passed. I
still sometimes think I've just felt his bushy tail against my leg
or heard his quiet meow. Maybe he never really left at all.

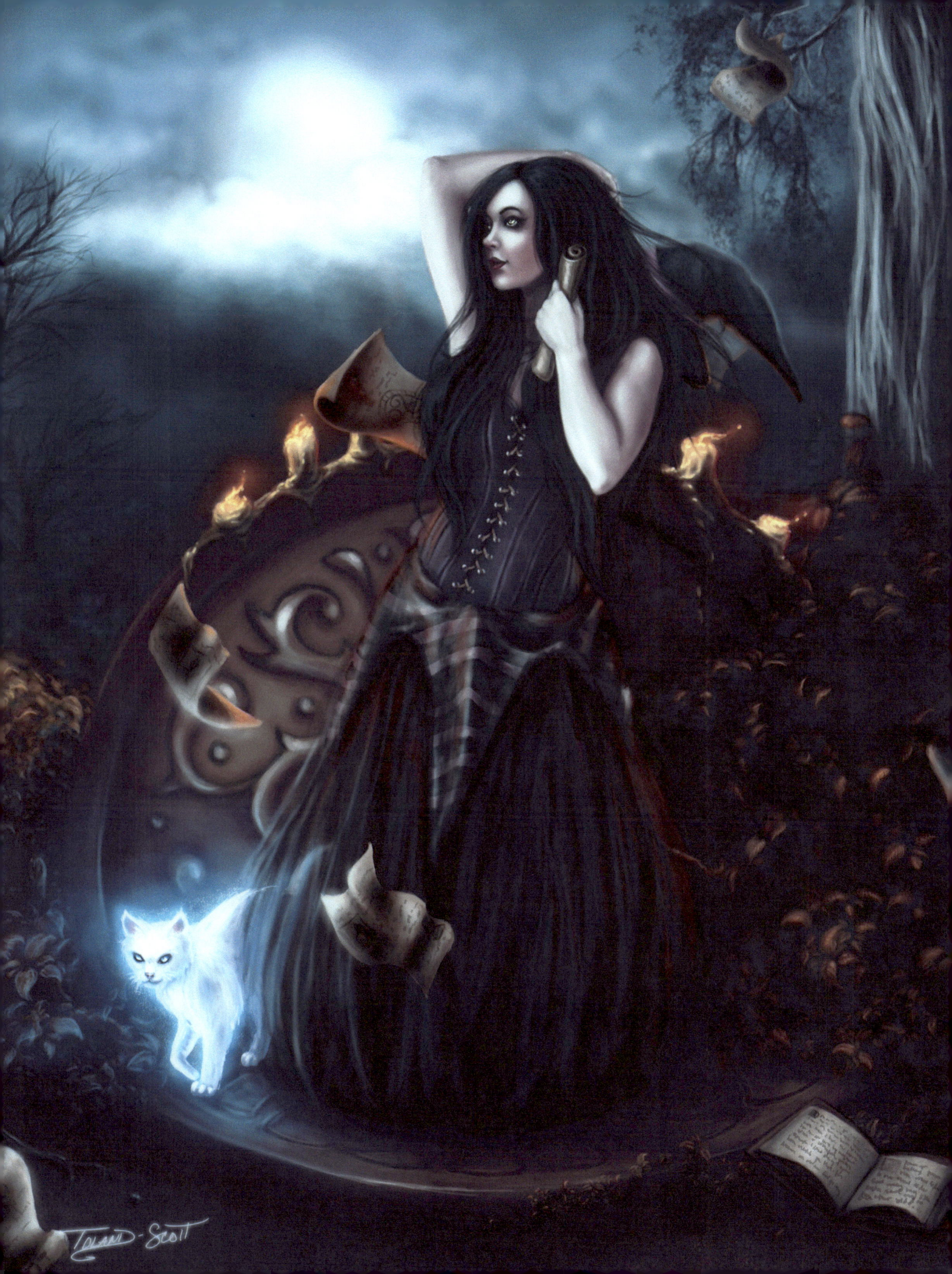

THE MARI-MORGANS

2013

Mari-morgans come from Welsh and Breton mythology
about siren-like creatures that trick men into
various bodies of water.
They lure them to the water with their beauty, and when
a little more persuasion is necessary, they show them
visions of underwater palaces and gardens.
A golden key rests in her hand - won't you jump in
and claim it?

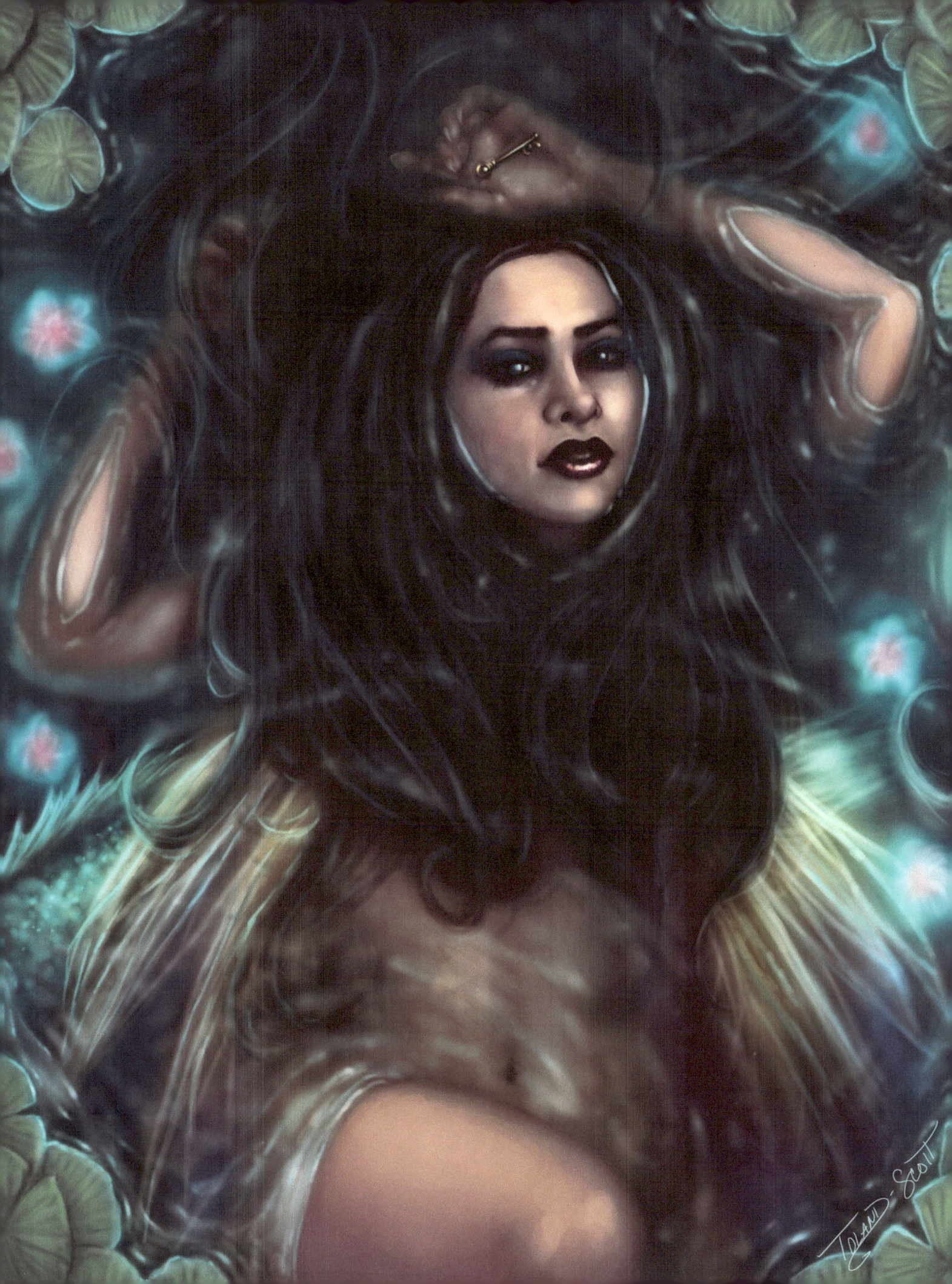

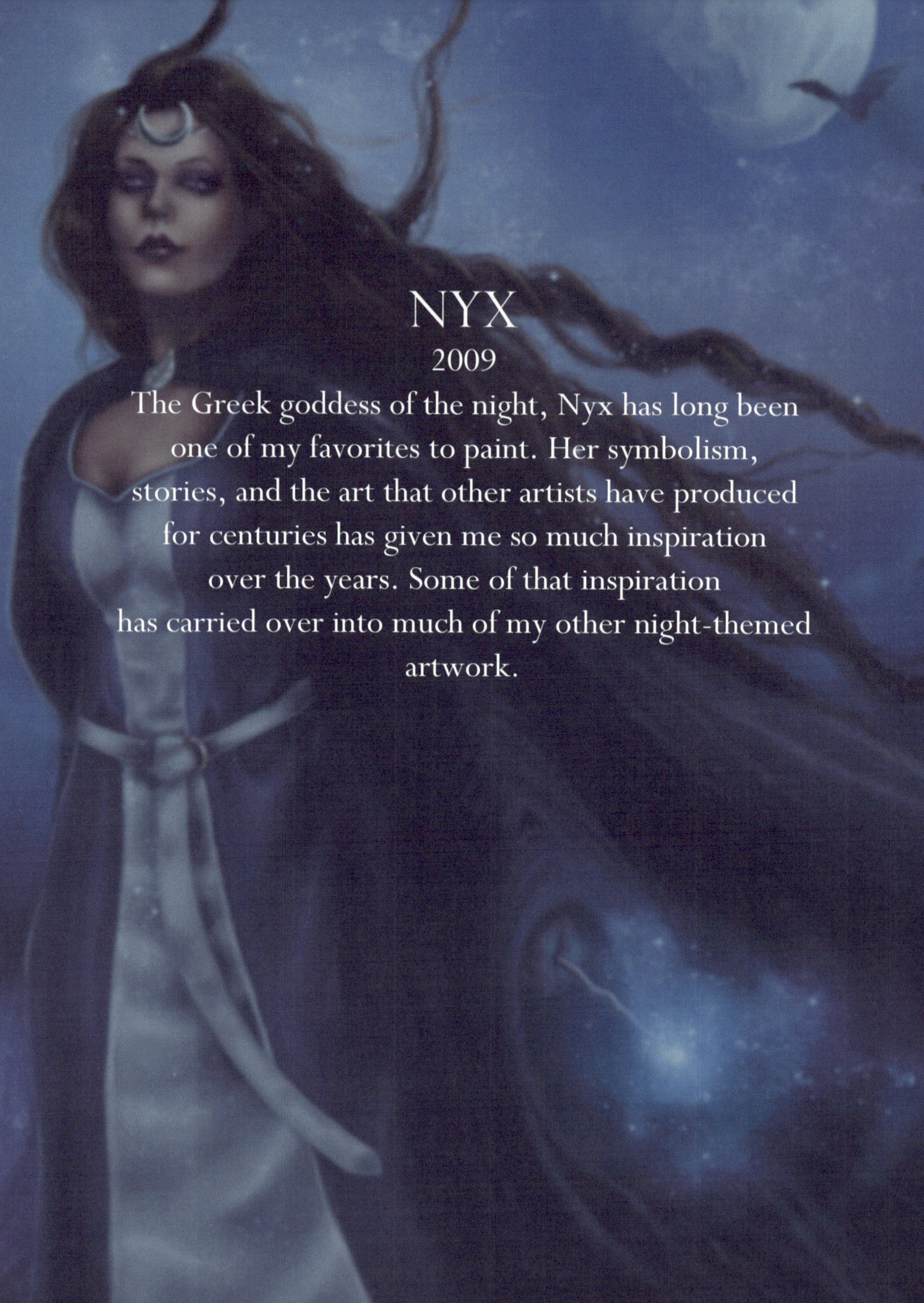

NYX

2009

The Greek goddess of the night, Nyx has long been one of my favorites to paint. Her symbolism, stories, and the art that other artists have produced for centuries has given me so much inspiration over the years. Some of that inspiration has carried over into much of my other night-themed artwork.

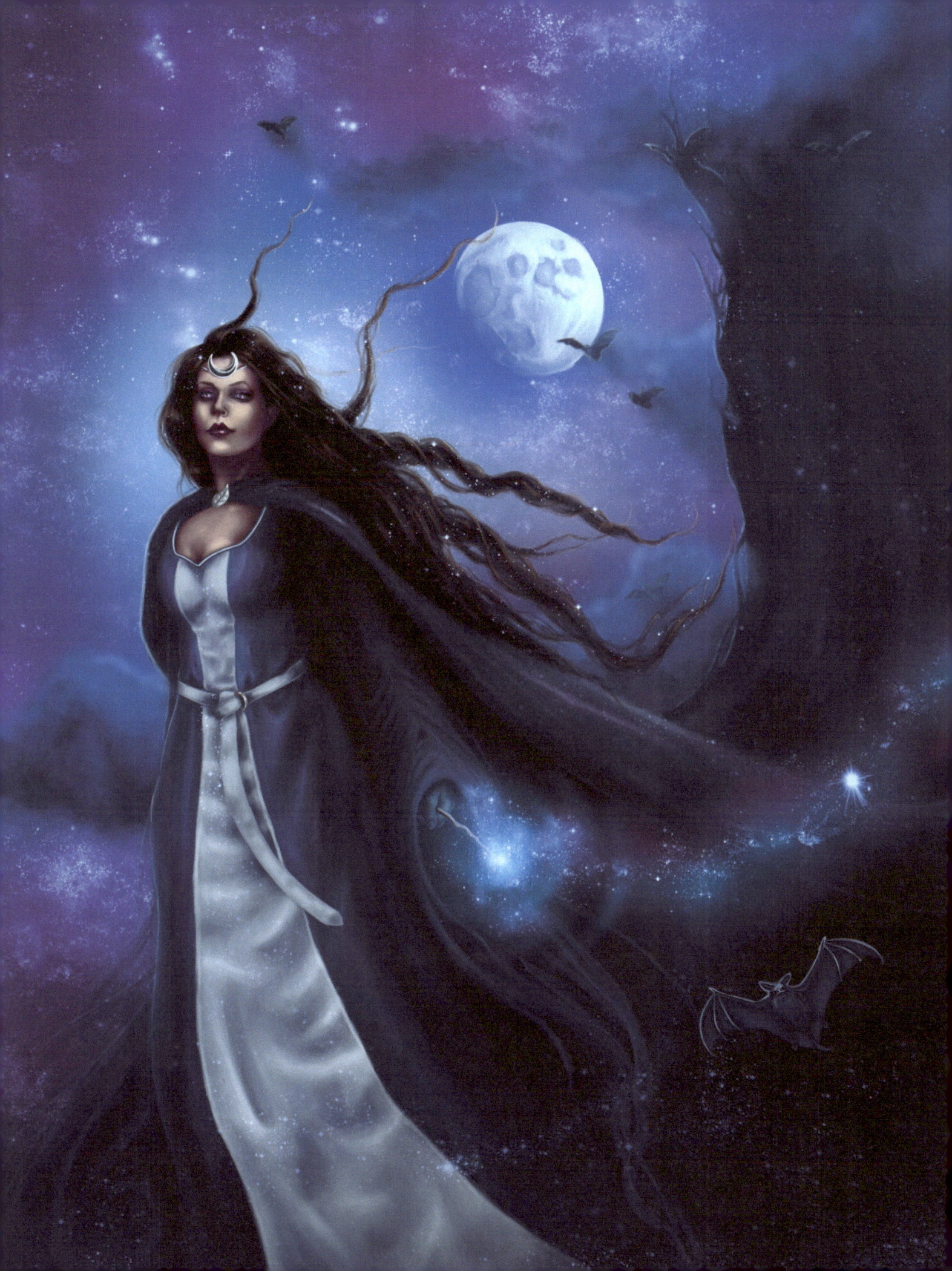

POSSESSED

2008

This painting is one of my favorite pieces that I've ever done.
It's not my greatest from a technical standpoint or
even an aesthetic one. What I love about it is that
everyone sees something different in it. For me, it was
about the duality that exists within each of us. Each person
is made up of varying amounts of "light and dark"
and in a way they couldn't exist without
each other.

Other people see different things - maybe sisters, or friends,
or even elements of nature, and more.

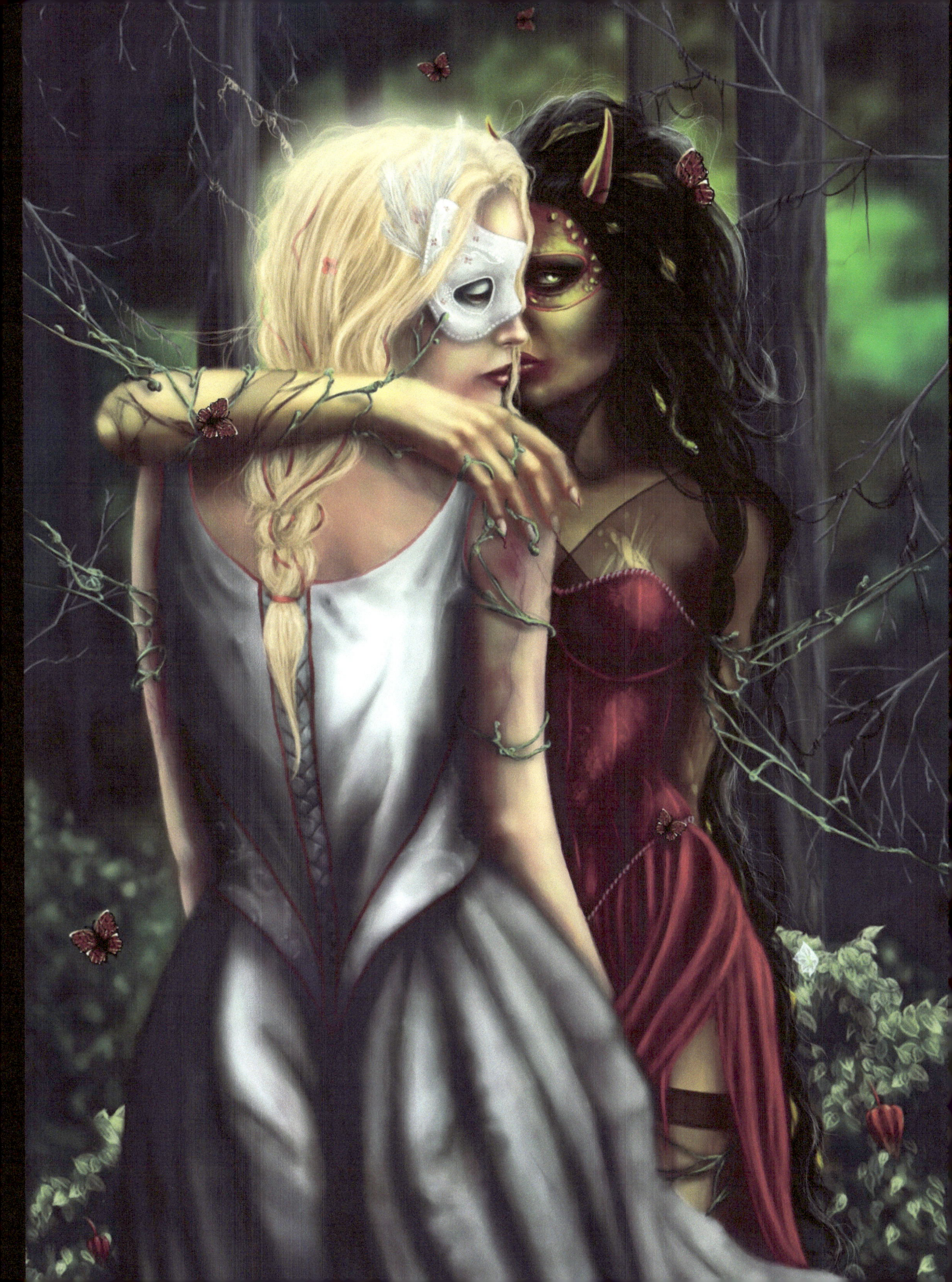

ADVENTURES IN ABSINTHIA

2012

For a long time I've been fascinated by the lore surrounding
absinthe and it's supposed hallucinogenic properties.
Many regular absinthe-drinkers from the 19th century
claimed to have visions of the green fairy after indulging
in the now expensive and difficult-to-find drink.
Most modern drinkers will find the legendary drink
induces no fairy visions - including this disappointed artist.

Alas, the absinthe of old was distilled through lead-copper
pipes, and the poets and artists of old were likely suffering
from a combination of lead poisoning and ingredients
that are no longer used in the preparation of the drink.

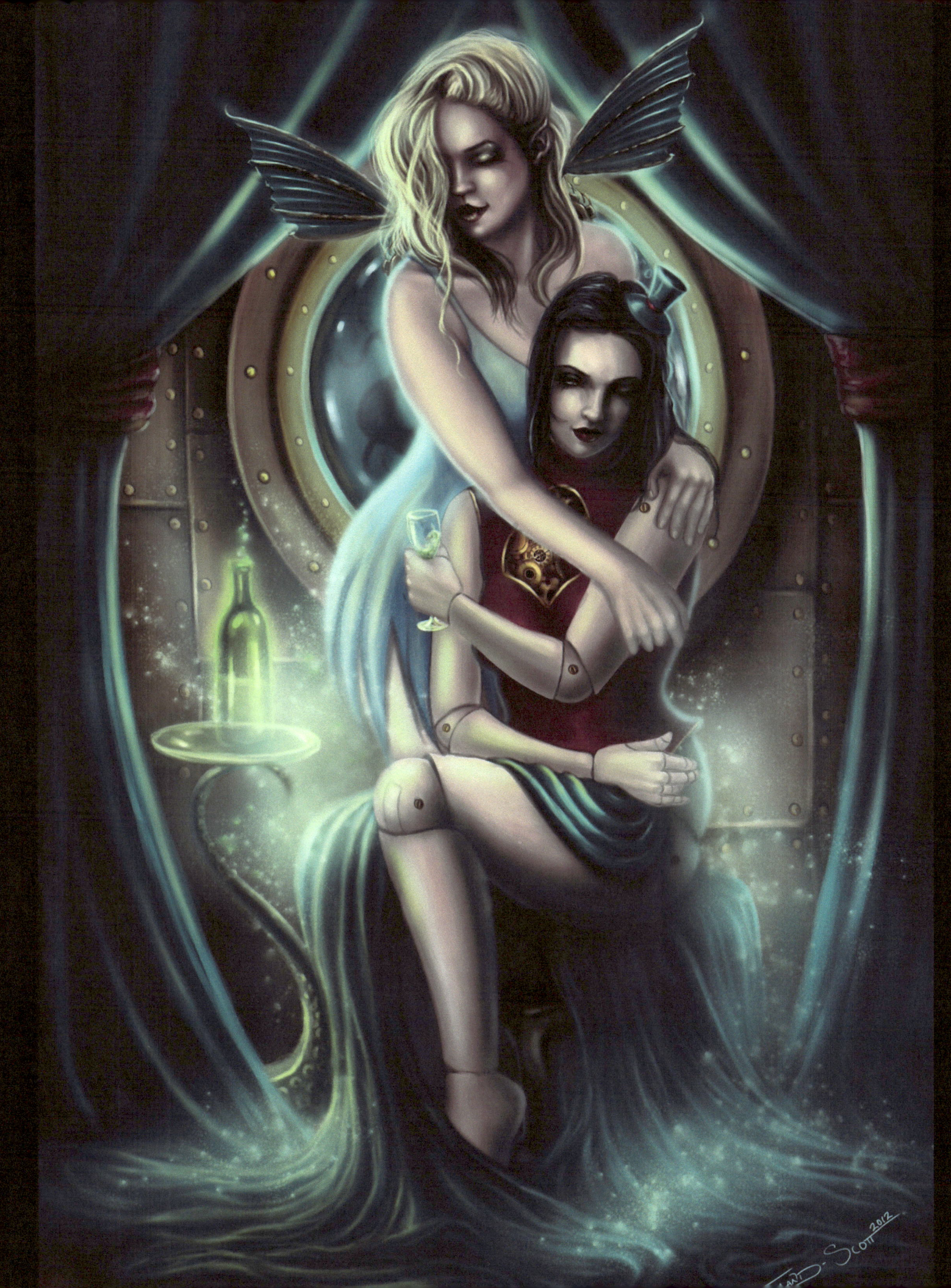

BLOODSTONE

2009

Bloodstone has been one of my most successful vampire pieces to date. I originally painted this as a simple character portrait, but I eventually made the decision to put her into my general portfolio. Not long after I made that decision, Flame Tree Publishing contracted the rights to print her in a calendar and a book of vampire art.

Not bad for a little warm-up piece!

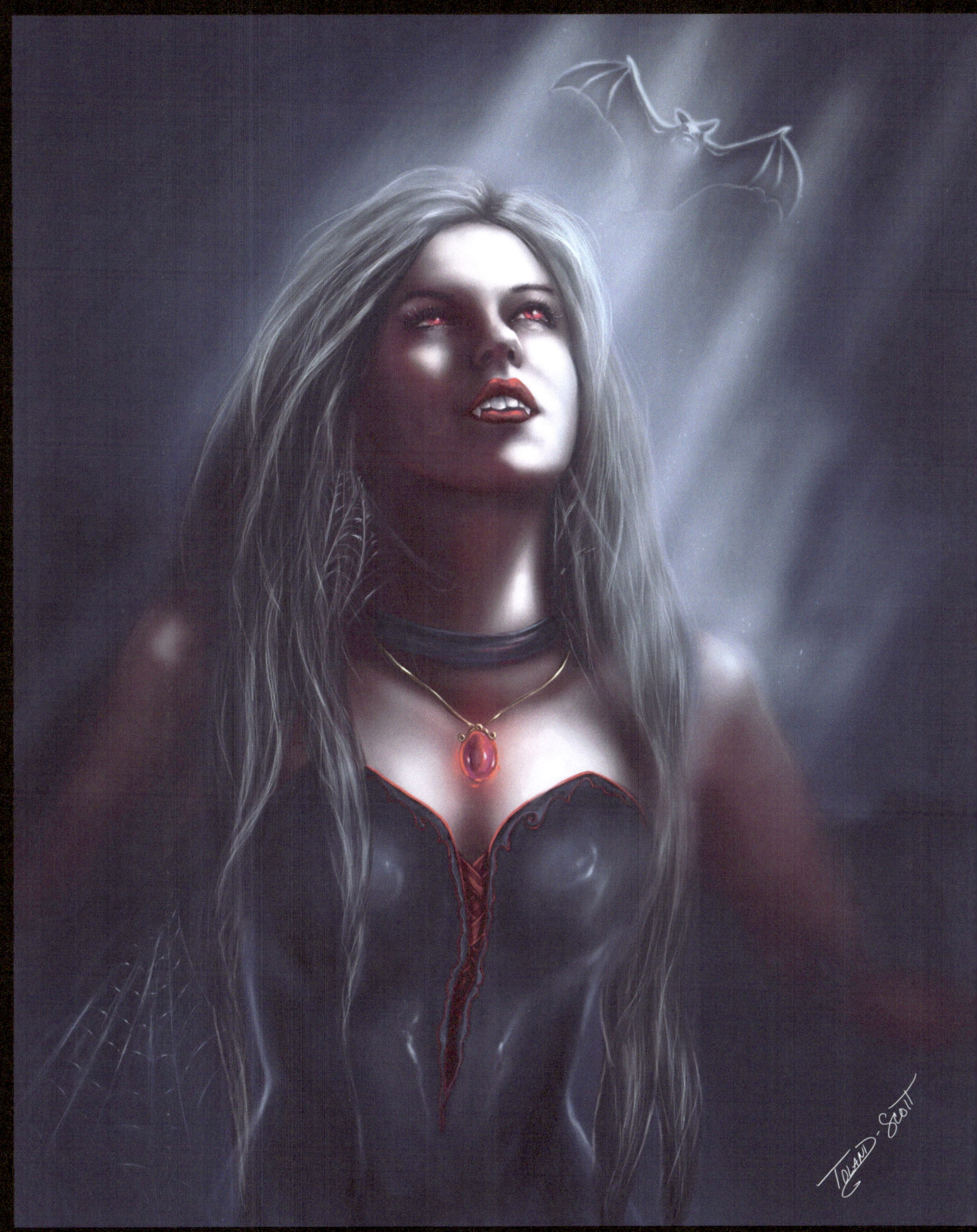

EXTINGUISHED

2008

Back in 2008 my first official studio had just opened up. I'd decided to try alternating between sweet, light-hearted paintings of fairies and elves and Gothic, blood-sucking vamps to keep a balance. I think, looking back at my work during this period, I should have just stuck with making blood-sucking vamps, because it's clear to me that's where my passion really was.

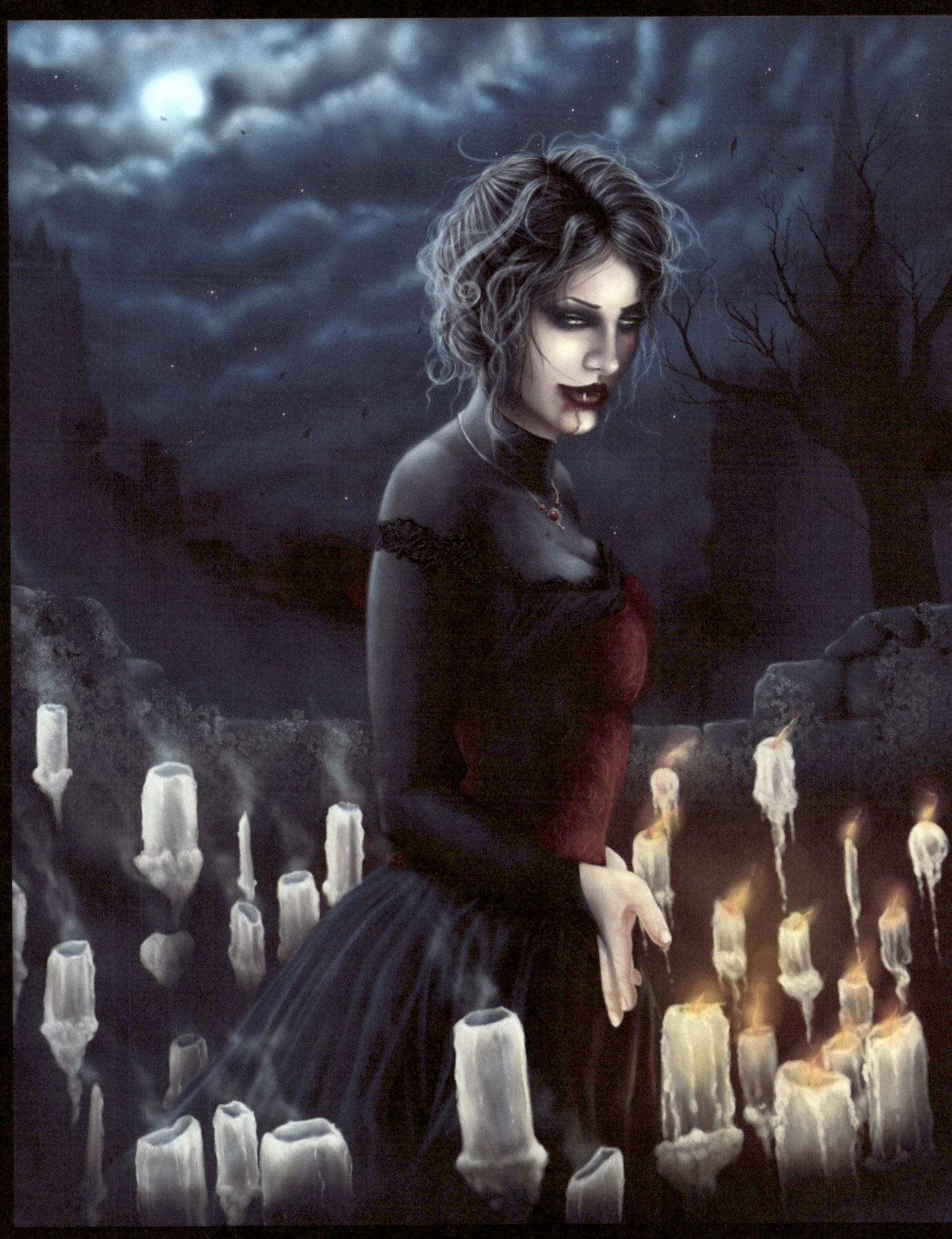

HAUNTED MOON

2007

It's funny how often I set out to make something sweet and inoffensive and instead I end up in undead lady territory with no idea of how I got there.

"Haunted Moon" is another example of that. I had intended to make a perfectly sweet fairy with a generic moon background and some crystalline elements.

Instead I made a ghost pirate.

It's almost the same thing… at least there's a moon in the background.

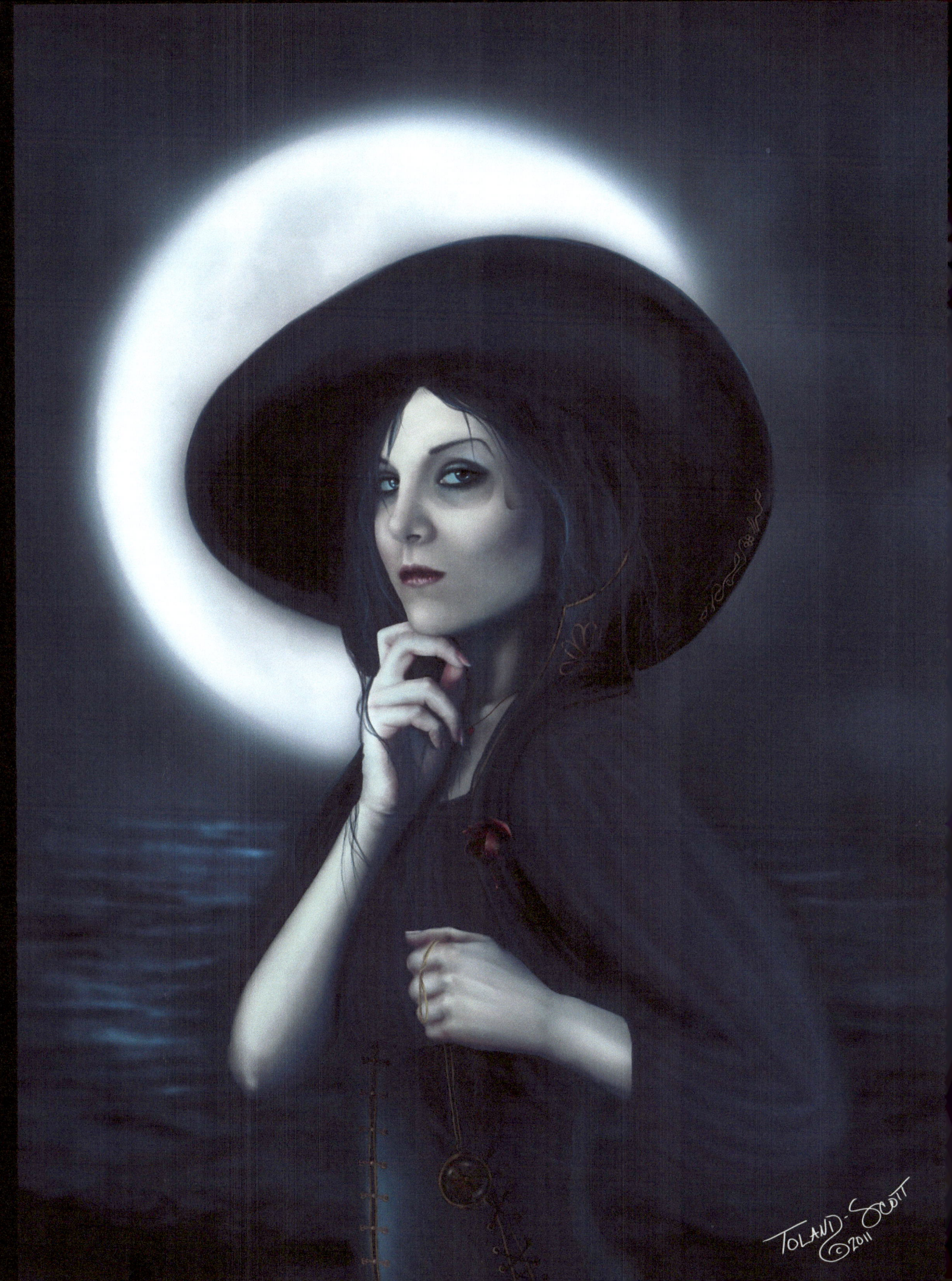

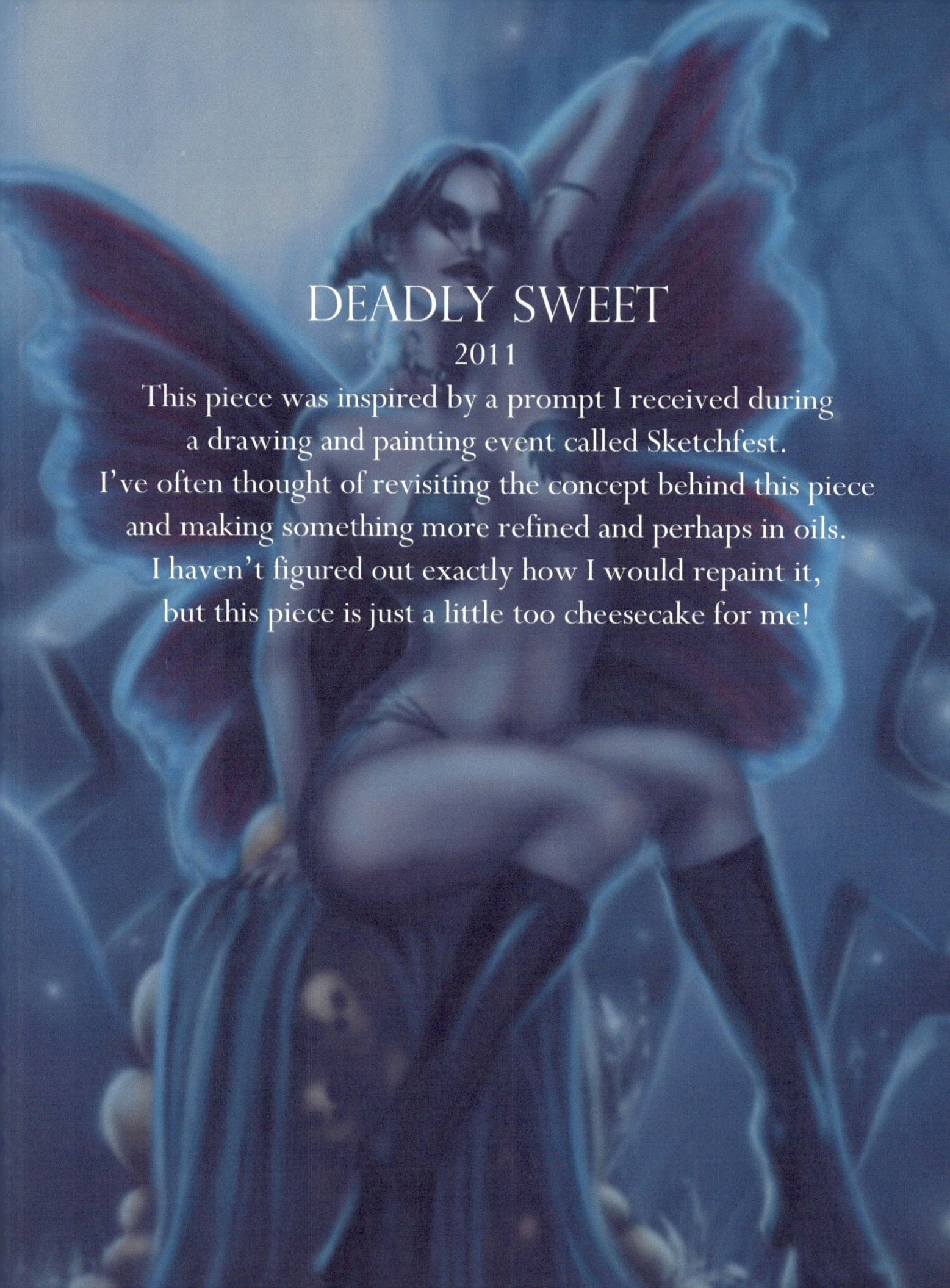

DEADLY SWEET

2011

This piece was inspired by a prompt I received during
a drawing and painting event called Sketchfest.
I've often thought of revisiting the concept behind this piece
and making something more refined and perhaps in oils.
I haven't figured out exactly how I would repaint it,
but this piece is just a little too cheesecake for me!

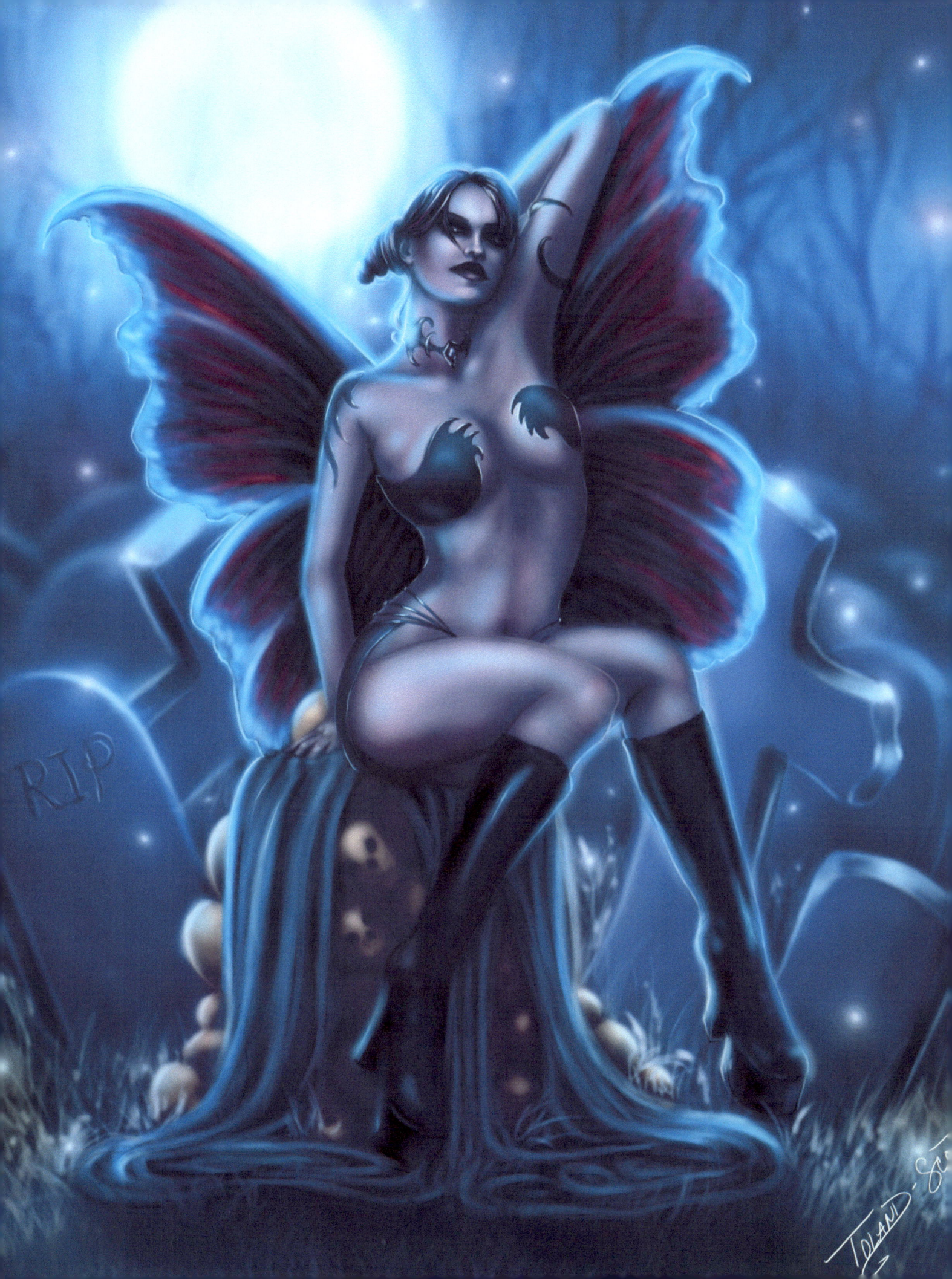

MIDNIGHT IN THE OUBLIETTE

2008

I painted this piece and the next one right after I made my
decision to leave art school. It was not an easy
decision to make and I worried about what I would
do with my life if I didn't have a degree.
But I worried more about staying, losing years of my time,
and sinking tens of thousands of dollars into
student debt for a degree I've ultimately
never needed.

Sometimes we just have to do what feels right, even
if it also feels terrifying.

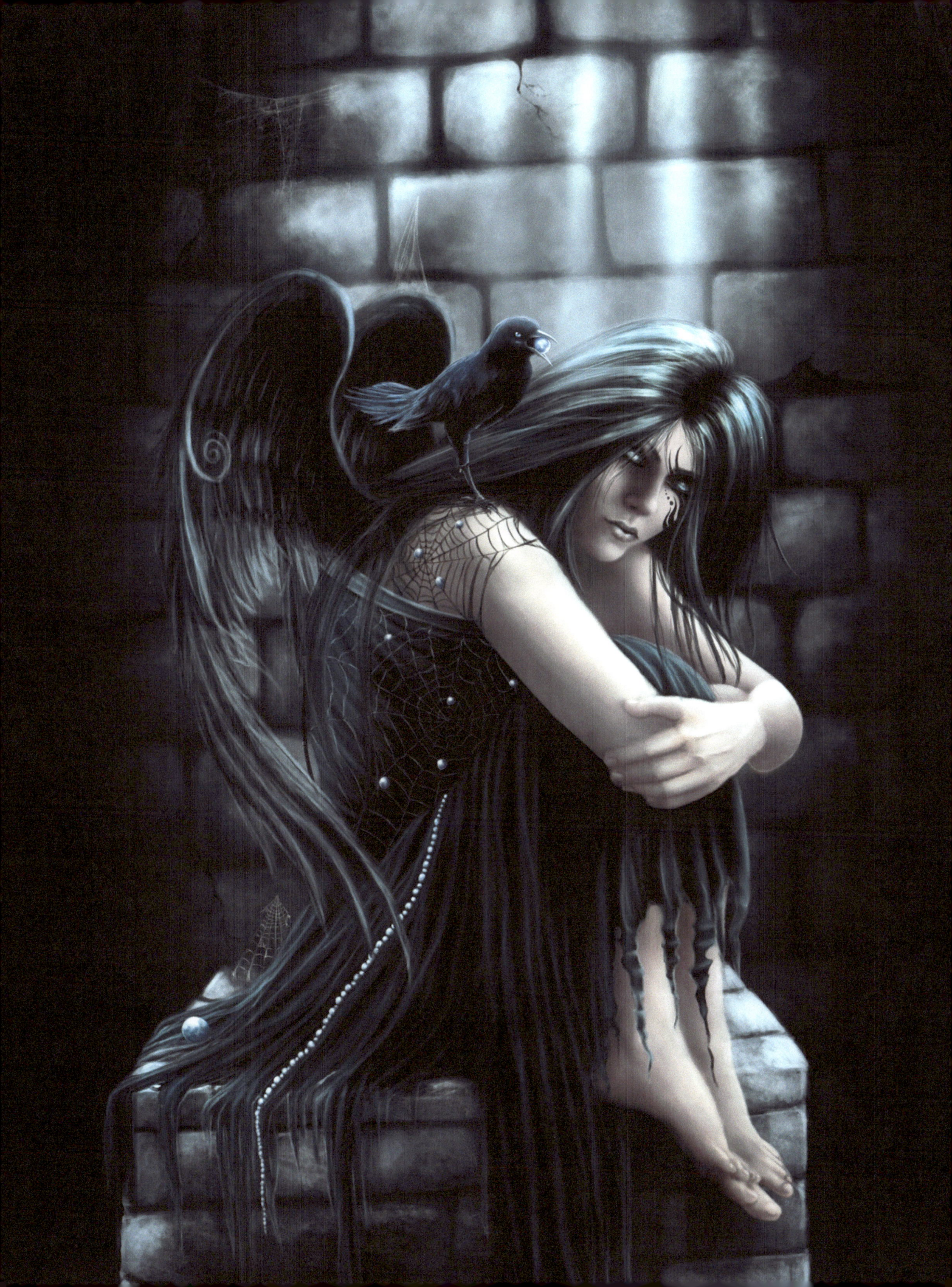

FORGOTTEN

2008

In my final months at art school, I painted Forgotten and Midnight in the Oubliette. I think they were definitely a reflection of how I was feeling. Isolated from my family and friends, lost, completely in the dark about my future and where I was going after dropping out of art school. Those were some dark times.

A month after I finished these pieces, I'd open my first real art studio and things would suddenly become a lot clearer, but I had no way of knowing what the future held.

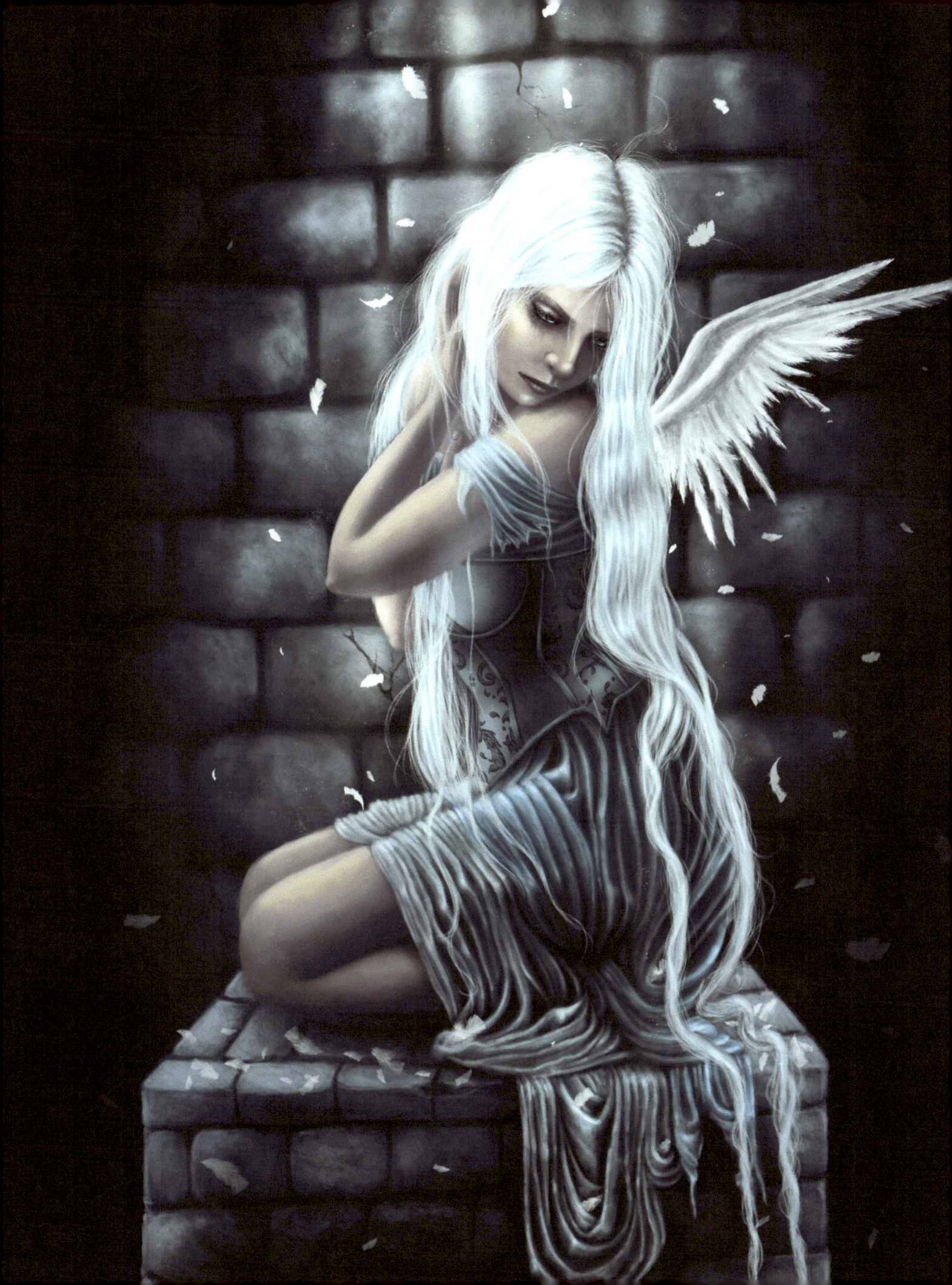

HER GHOST

2005

Once upon a time I was a baby artist with no idea about resolution or making images that were large enough to be printed on actual paper at appreciable sizes. I've already doubled the size of this piece and it won't even fill this letter-sized page. I don't dare stretch it further - it might be totally unrecognizable if I did.

During that time, I unfortunately hit on some cool ideas and I still enjoy some of the art that I made back then. I wanted to include this piece, and I hope you'll forgive the small size of it.

If I had a time machine, I'd slap me.

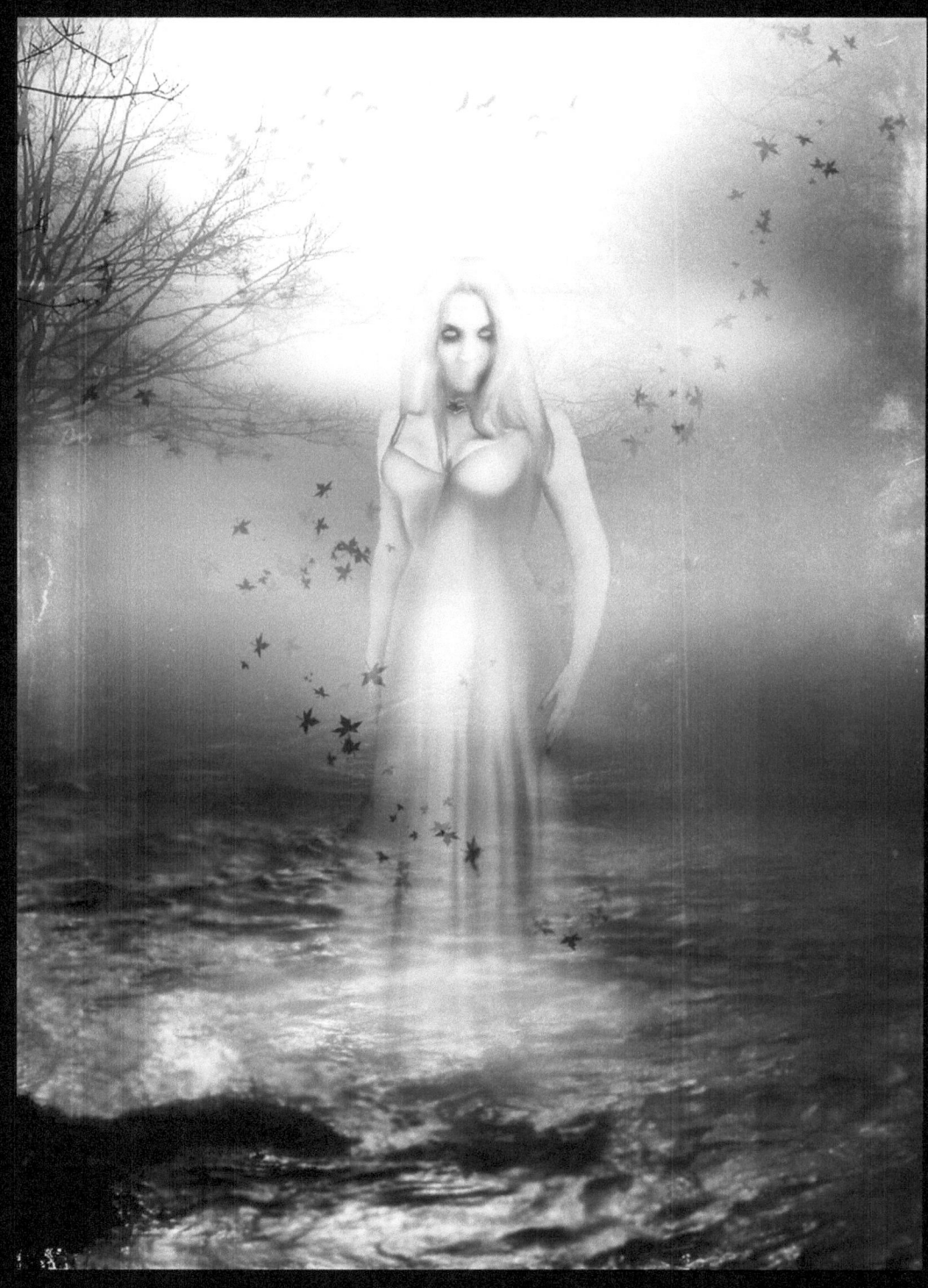

LAMIA

2014

One of the last pieces I ever painted digitally, Lamia was originally intended for a book of skull imagery, but I was never satisfied with the painting and decided not to submit it.

I love the mythology of Lamia - a cursed snake-woman creature that eats children, usually after being driven mad by her grief. I've seen some really beautiful Lamia paintings, too. But after three separate attempts, I still haven't managed to capture her exactly the way I would like to.

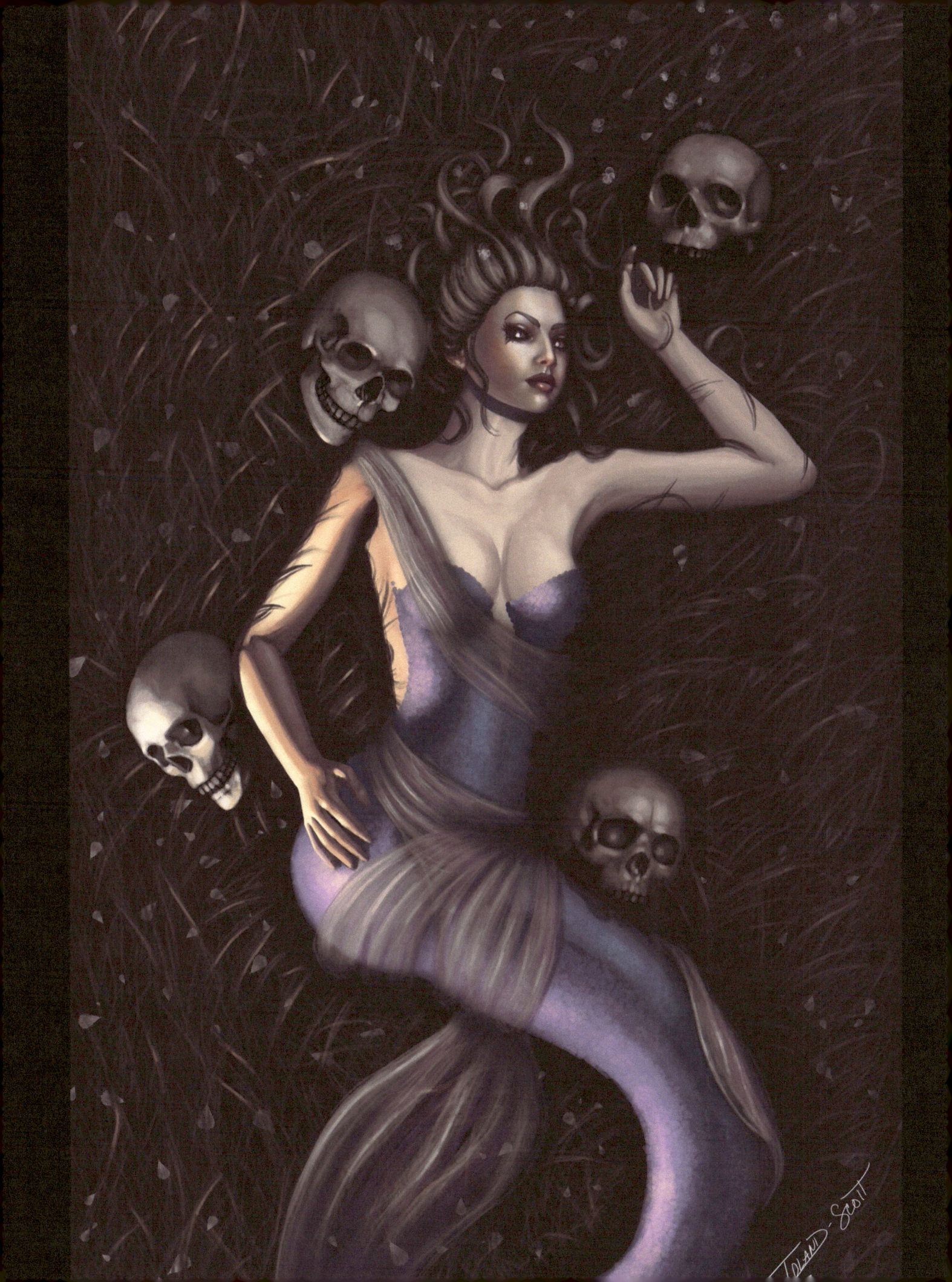

LATET ANGUIS IN HERBA

2013

I'm sure you're familiar with the phrase, "a snake in the grass", but if you're not an American and haven't encountered it before, it roughly means that someone isn't what they seem.

Generally, it means they're preying on someone.

I wonder what this "fairy" is preying on?

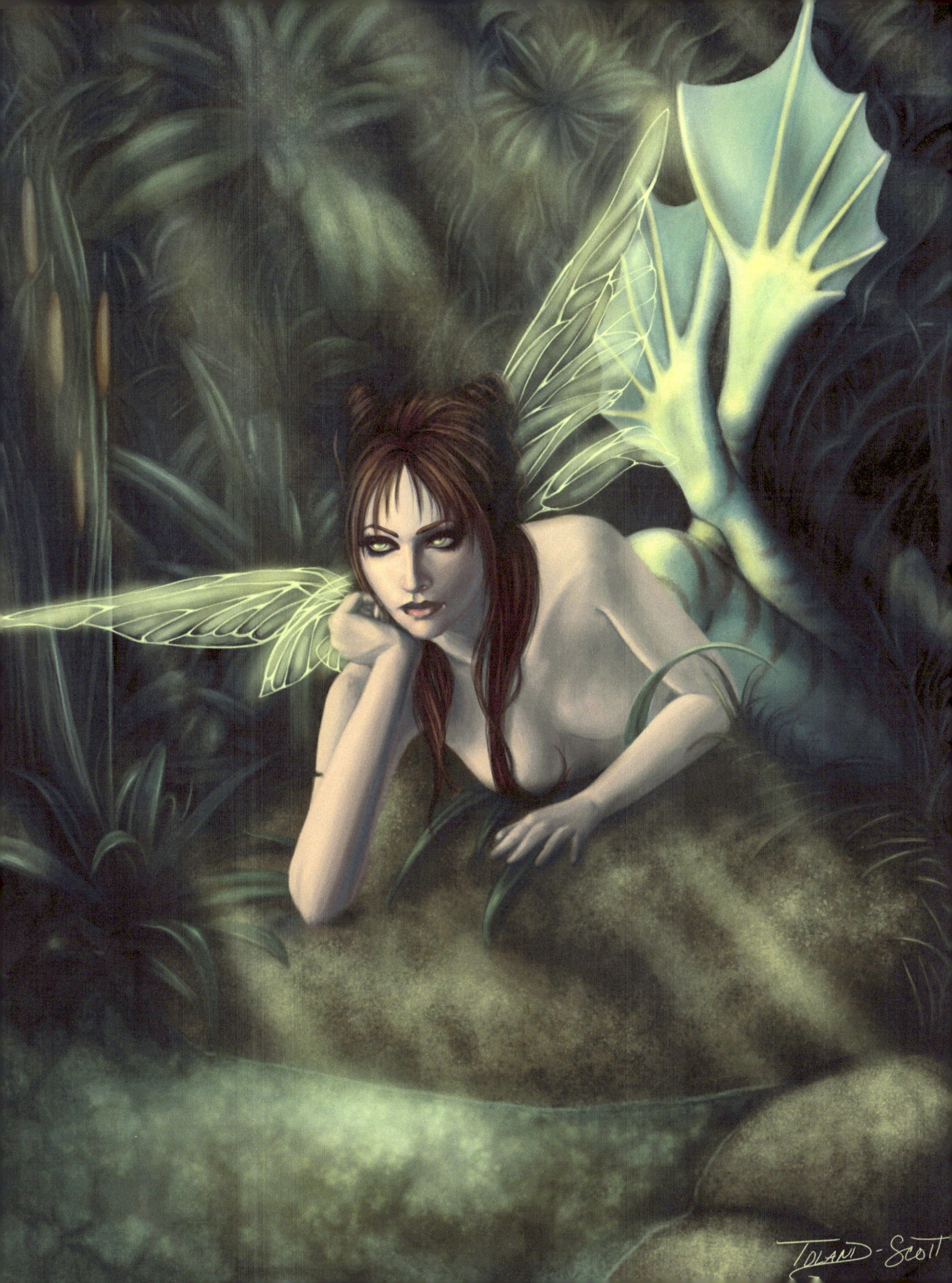

MY ONLY FRIEND
2009

Sometimes life takes us to new places, and sometimes
in those new places it can be difficult to find
new friends. When you work from home it
becomes especially difficult to meet new people.
I've moved a lot during my career and have made few
"real life" friends over the years. Often the only people
I know are people my husband has met at his job.

It's kind of odd, and sometimes lonely, but I have a lot of
pets and work to keep me busy. It's definitely not
a lifestyle that most people would appreciate,
but I like it.

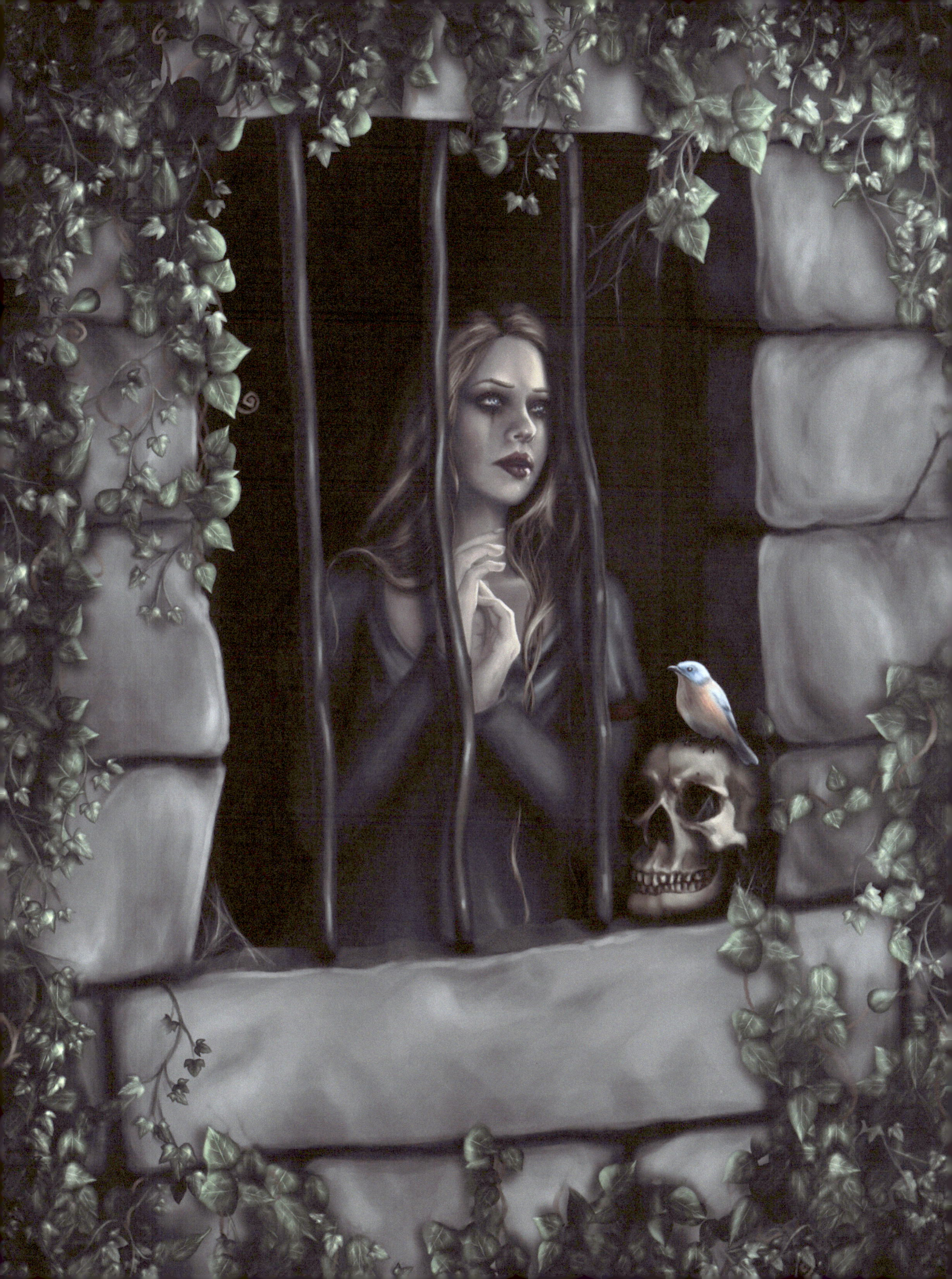

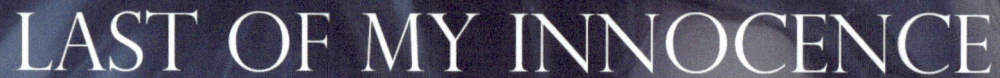

LAST OF MY INNOCENCE
2012
A dark angel, still bleeding from her fall, clutches the last white feather of her wings. This painting was a response to various things that were going on in the world at the time. I think it's important to hold onto whatever childlike joy you can, especially when you're an adult. The world is simply too dark without it.

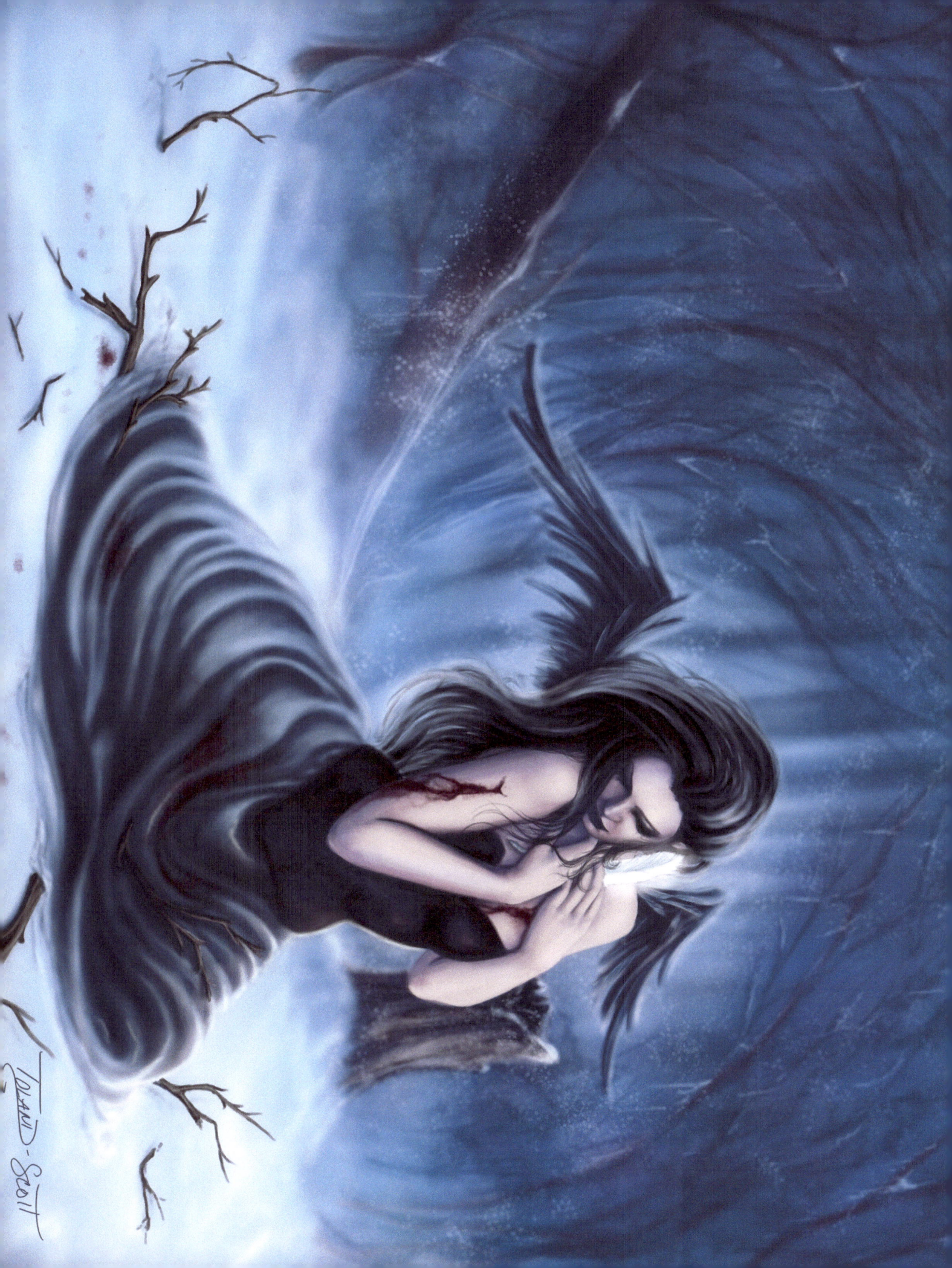

MALDITA
2011

In the summer of 2011 I packed up my computer and
went to my grandmother's house for a week. I'd had a baby
that spring and really needed some time to paint,
so for a week she took care of my son and I painted as much
as I could.

Three paintings were born that week - this one, and the
two paintings that follow.

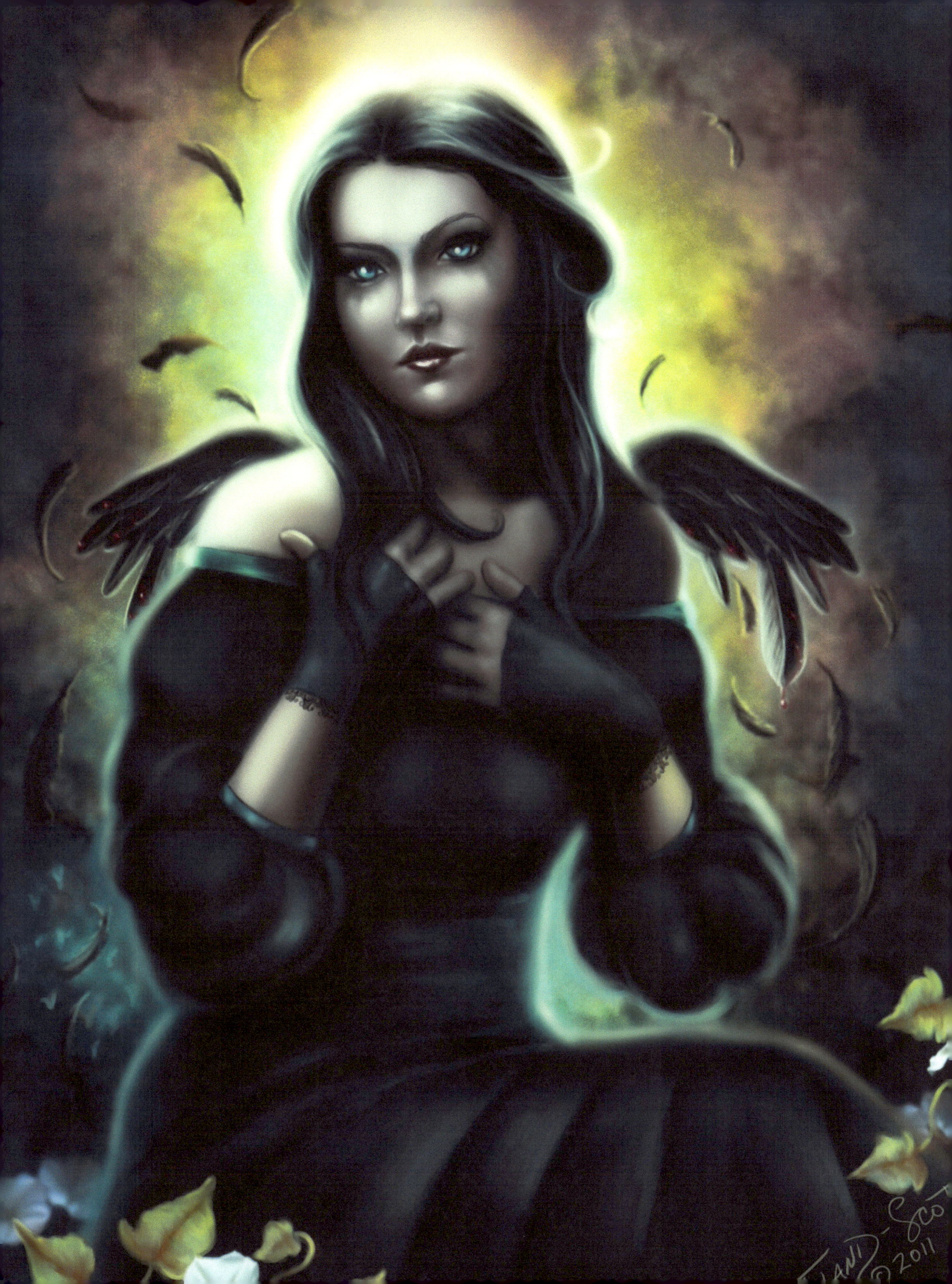

THE WEEPING ANGELS

2011

Ever since I was a child I've had an uncanny feeling
about angel statues. You can only imagine my
elation about a certain TV show that hit upon
my childhood phobia like a hammer striking a nail.
For the first time I didn't feel like I was alone, a weird
little girl with a strange idea and a wild imagination.
No, someone else thought the same thing.

The things move whenever you're not looking.

Strangely enough, I painted this before I ever watched
that season.

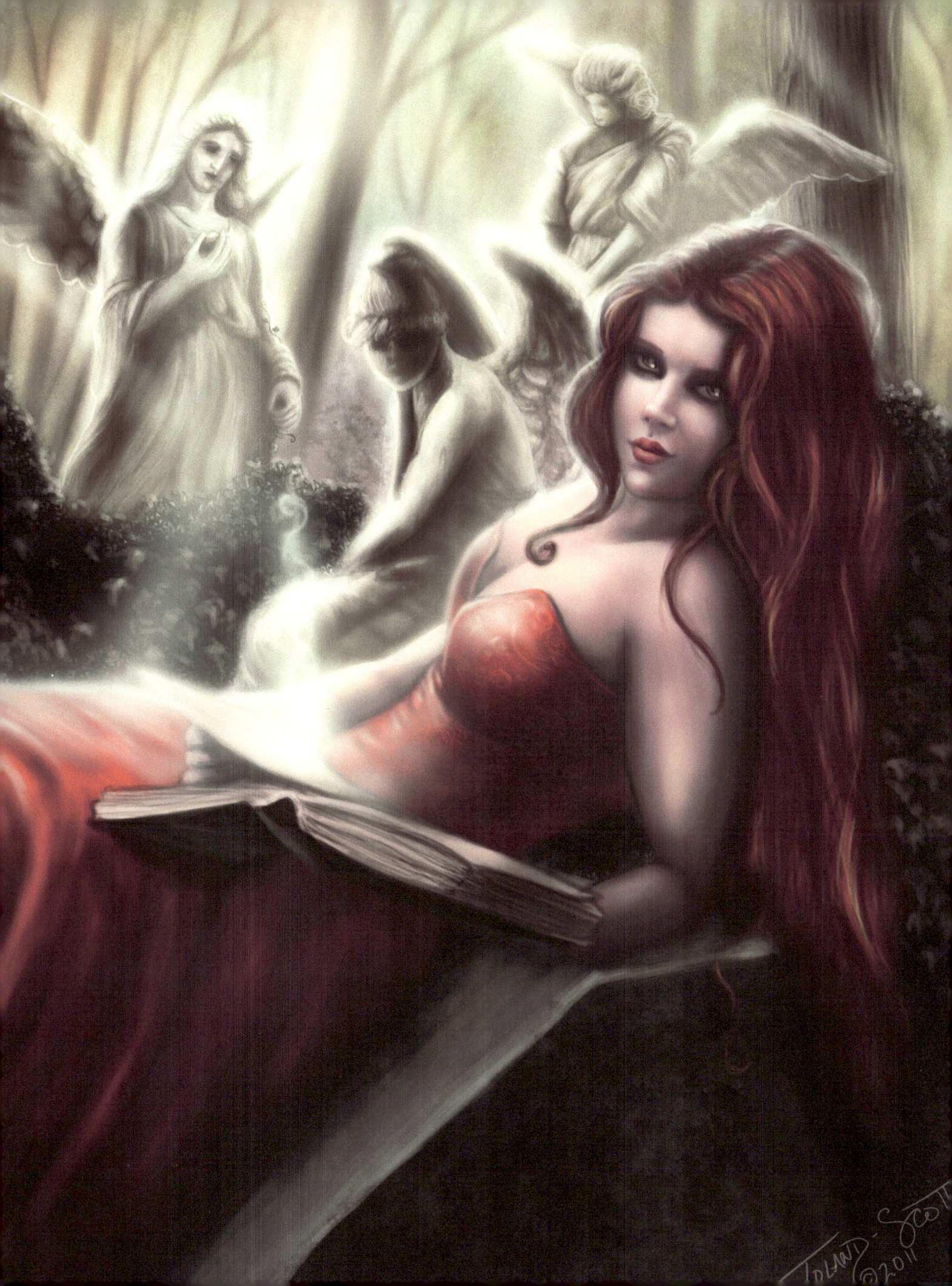

THE WOUNDED ANGEL

2011

Hugo Simberg painted his painting, "The Wounded Angel",
in 1903. Since then it has inspired innumerable artists,
musicians, and writers, and I am no exception.
Hugo was recovering from meningitis when he painted
his painting, and some people think the blindfolded
angel is allegorical for the light sensitivity meningitis causes.
I suffer from ocular migraines - strange painless migraines
that cause visual distortions and, when they are
extremely bad, mild visual hallucinations.
I can relate to his angel. Sometimes I just want to wrap
my head up and be carried.

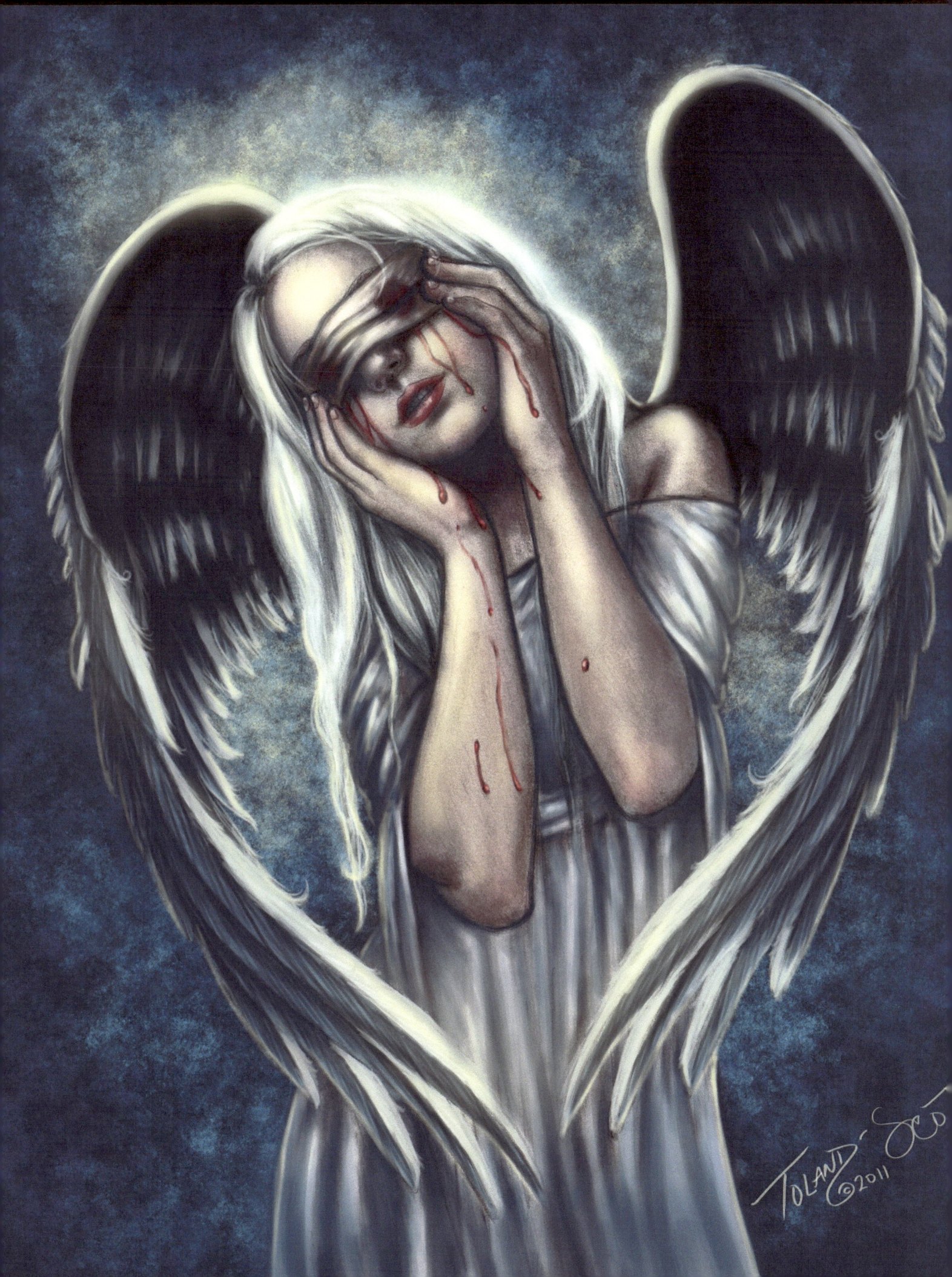

LAST ROSE OF SUMMER

2012

I used to live in Montana, and often it would snow before
the last roses had wilted and dropped their petals.
It made me a little sad to see the beautiful frost-bitten
flowers still clinging to their thorny stems, but
there was also something beautiful about the roses
blanketed in frost and snow.

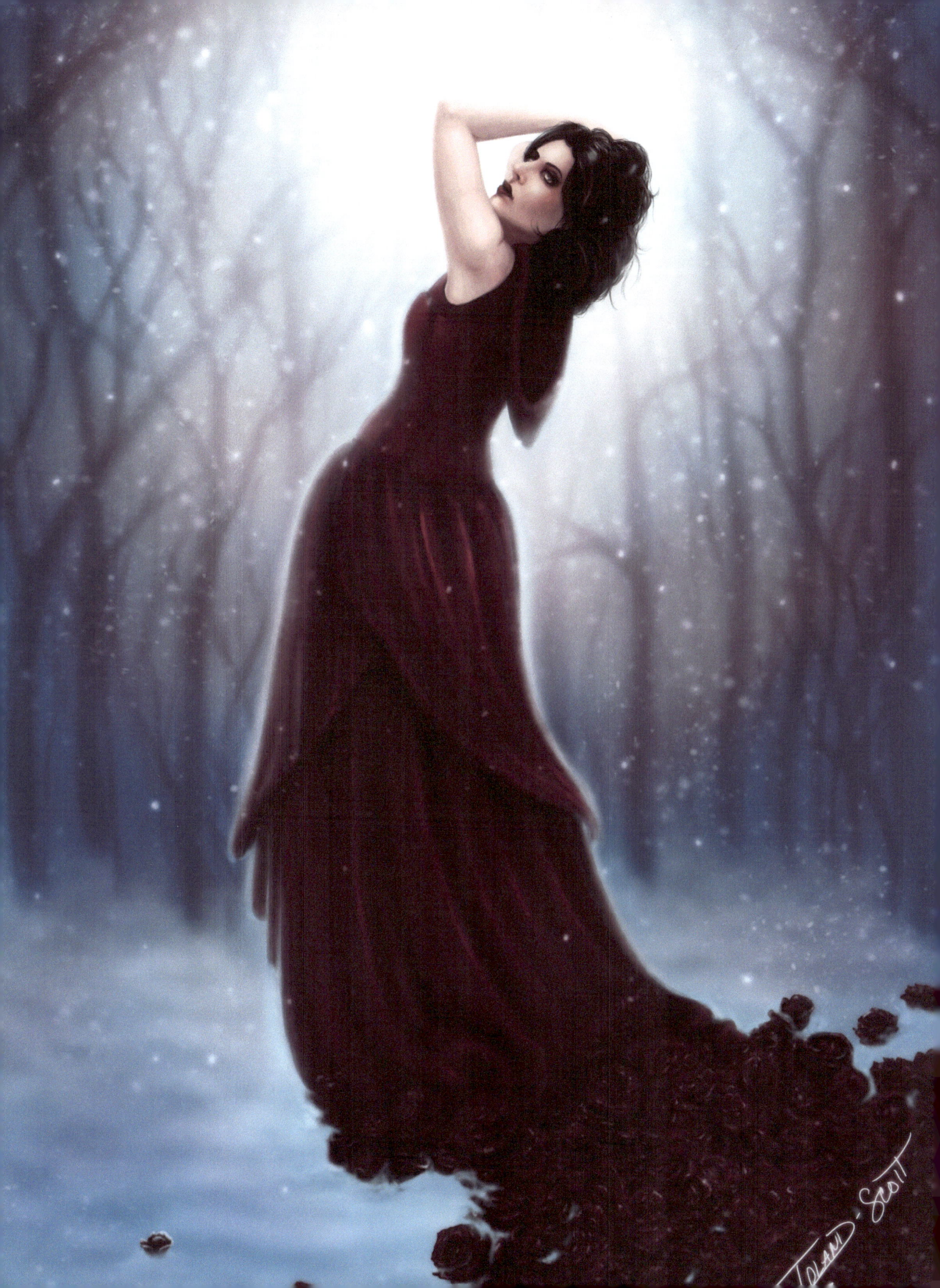

More books available from www.titoland.com

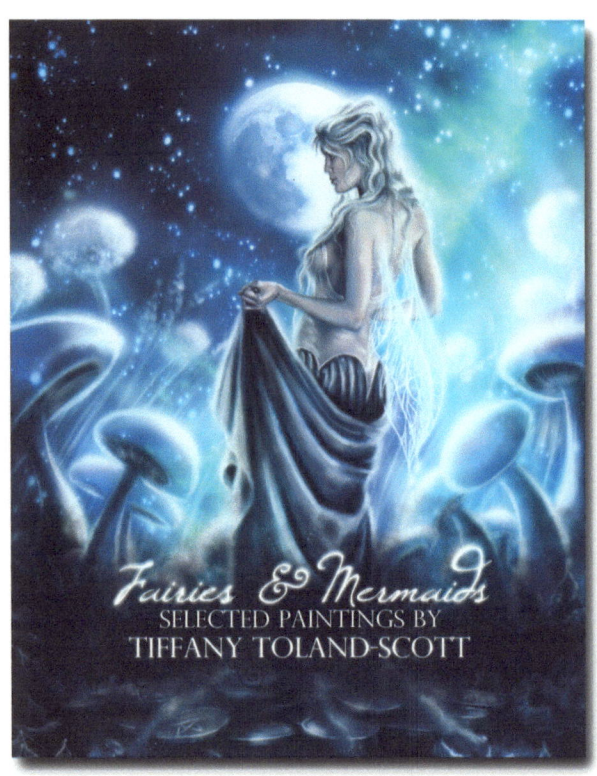

Fairies & Mermaids

2015

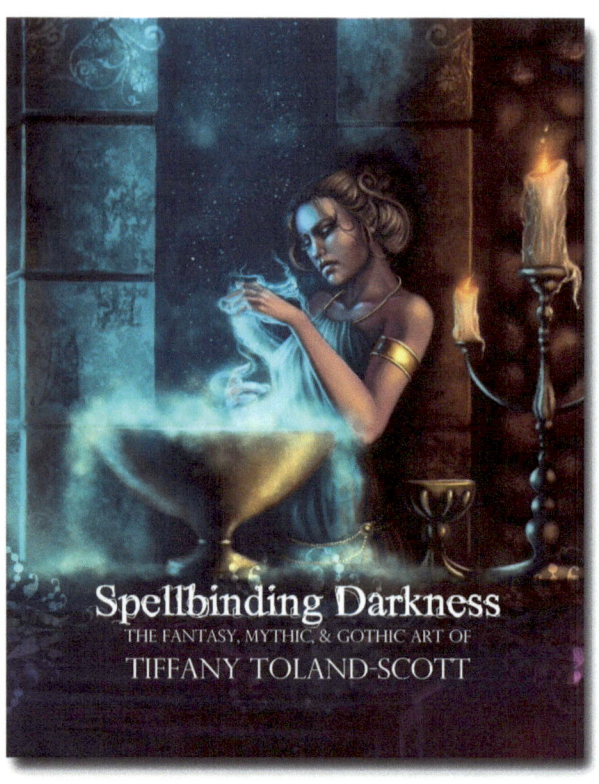

Spellbinding Darkness

2015

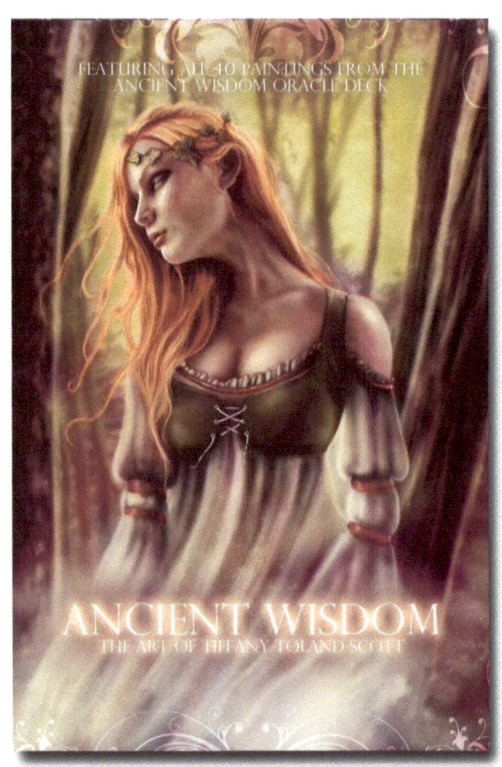

Ancient Wisdom

2013

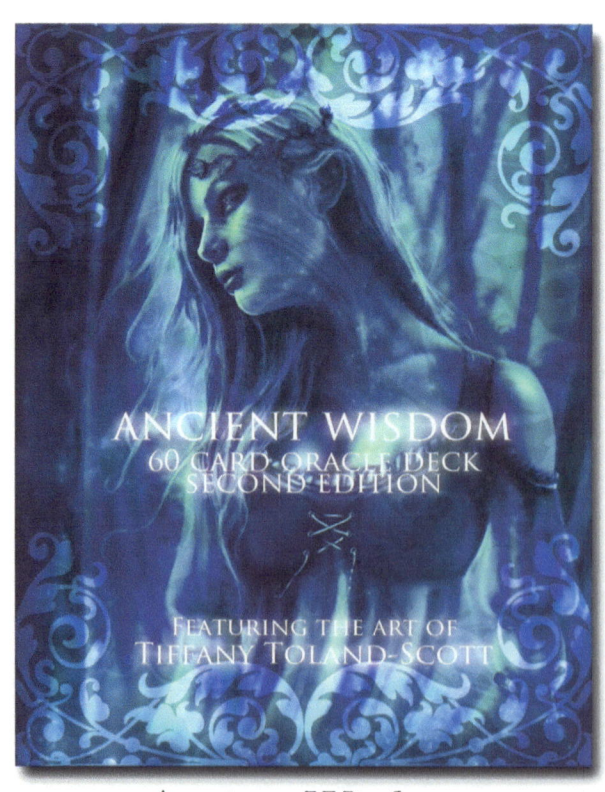

Ancient Wisdom
60-card Oracle Deck

2013 & 2015

DON'T MISS THE COMPANION COLORING BOOK!

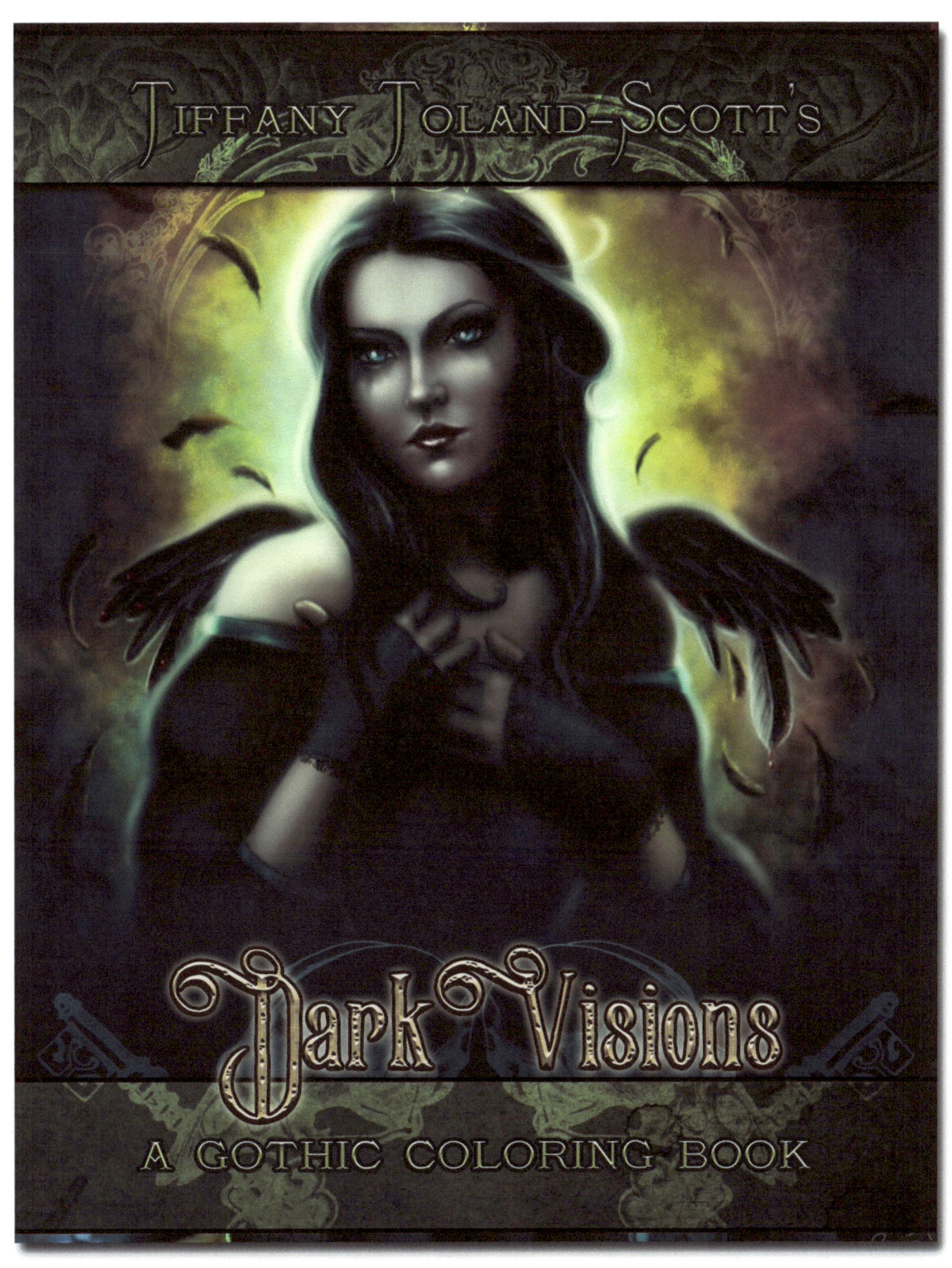

AVAILABLE NOW!

Want more coloring fun?

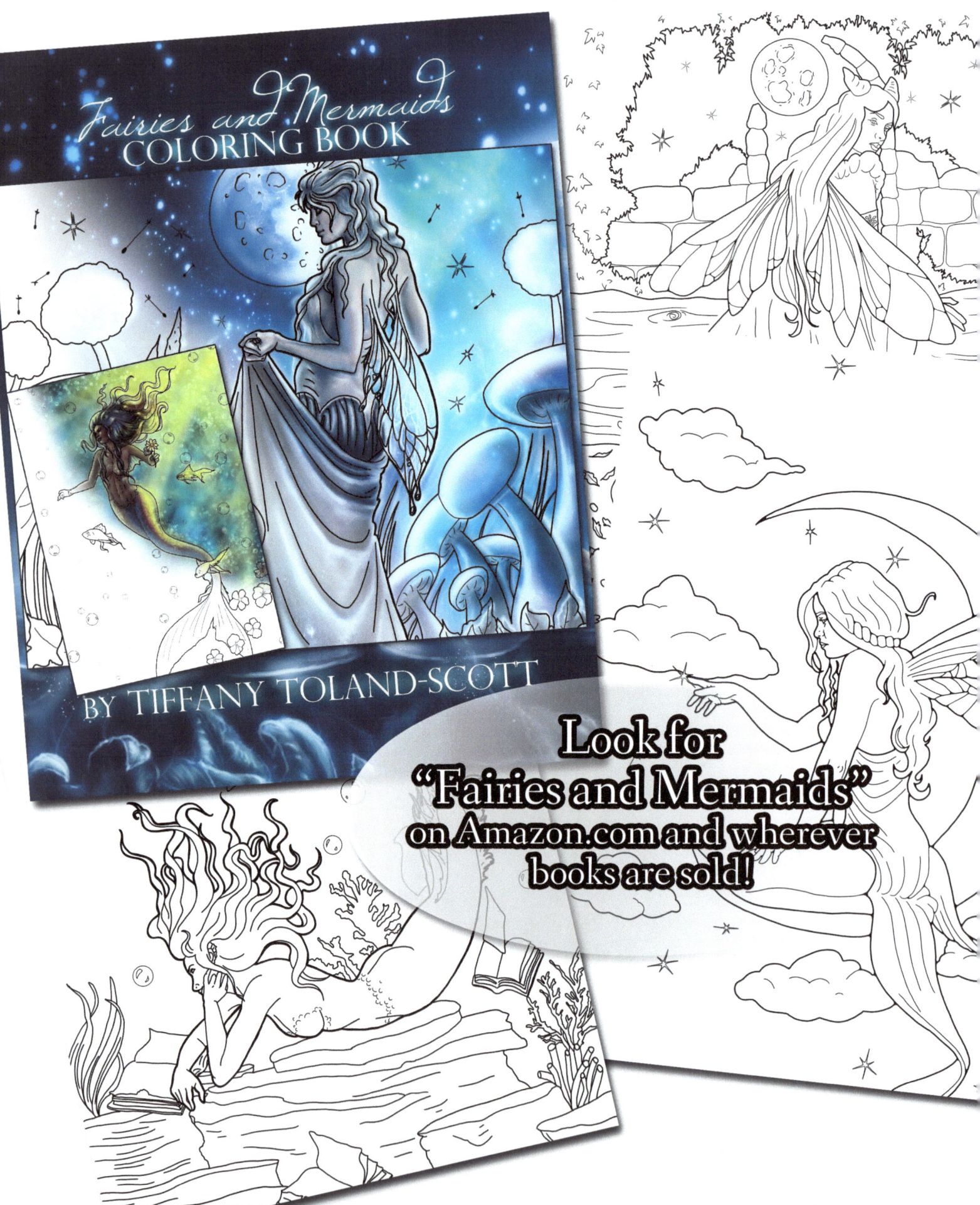